THE 11TH COMMANDMENT

By Dr. David Trucker

DORRANCE
PUBLISHING CO
EST. 1920
PITTSBURGH, PENNSYLVANIA 15238

Dorrance Publishing Co
585 Alpha Drive
Pittsburgh, PA 15238
Visit our website at www.dorrancebookstore.com

ISBN: 978-1-4809-5496-0
eISBN: 978-1-4809-5473-1

Introduction

After completing the book, *A Touch of the Underworld* the story of my family's role in the development of the Cleveland syndicate, I have been asked by many to relate the story of my own life, which even I can't believe as I reflect upon the events.

If the content of this book deviates from complete veracity, please remember that I am now eighty-seven years of age with an element of dementia, and therefore exact objectivity is clouded again by mental illness, medications, and frequent trips to the bathroom, not necessarily all at nighttime.

Also, I again ask you not to judge me unless you have walked in my moccasins for many miles. I wish to point out that we are all products of our heredity and environment, and I also have the additional handicap of being fearless and brainless, without the ability to recognize barriers.

I really haven't aged too much in that I still like to chase girls, using my cane, but the problem being that once I catch them, I don't know what to do. Likewise, please bear in mind that some of the details in this book are completely factual, some are embellished, and some have an element of sheer fabrication. It is up to you to figure out which is which. Let's begin with that remembrance, but also bear in mind that an anachronism must be excused due to senility.

Chapter 1

So what's the story behind this kid who grew up in an underworld setting and ultimately became a successful military and civilian surgeon, teacher and medical administrator (and hopefully a successful writer in his terminal years)?

As a small child, to the amusement of all, I was known as an acute businessman. For example, I would not trade away a nickel in exchange for two dimes, because the nickel was larger and thus worth more. Repeated attempts to reverse this thought process were not successful. At age five I was away from the house for about four days. Upon my return I rummaged through all the wastebaskets, looking for something that might give me information as to what occurred while I was gone, as I did not want to miss anything.

The true highlight of my earlier years was my black mammy Laura, as my mother was very busy selling insurance and involved in religious activities. I am told that I would follow Laura around the house like a baby duck, quacking all the while and babbling any old thing. The history I actually remember at about age five, and which was confirmed by Laura later in my life, is when I would get upset about something, Laura would reply, "Uncle David is getting old."

At that time, black people could not only not own property in Cuyahoga Falls, Ohio where I lived, but they could not be in town after dark. This meant that Laura would take a bus from Akron to our home and change clothes in the basement to put on her white gown and thus subsequently deal with the daily activities. I apparently had followed her into the basement one morning, chirping all the way. While Laura was changing clothes with my accompaniment, my mother started to come down the basement steps. In the southern accent which I had developed and learned from Laura, I was told repeatedly afterwards that I shouted out, "Mama, you all no come down here 'cause Laura change her clothes."

Laura became a very important part of my life. The relationship produced permanent physical and emotional changes in my brain, so that in essence I have come to realize that although I may have a white face, I have a black heart and soul. To this day I have a deep love for the black race.

Other memorable events were secondary to the fact that the Googler sisters across the street had an icebox, not a refrigerator; they had not yet made the change. This meant that every day when the ice truck would come, I would be sure to be at the truck to receive a sliver of ice, which was probably analogous to having an ice cream cone. I also remember the old rag man coming up and down the street twice a week with his horse and buggy, shouting, "Papa dakes—ol' lad a ma dakes," (which translated means old rags and papers). Also, my job was to take the $50 rent check to the RC Hedden Realty Company on State Road, and at the same time pick up pumpernickel bread from Nichols Bakery, as we were only allowed to eat pumpernickel bread and no white sugar, in accordance with Amish tradition.

Truly the most memorable series of events occurred when I was six years of age. At that time the Communist Party was a legitimate political party in the United States, and was the diabolical enemy of the Catholic Church. With my mother's primary role in the Catholic Church at that time, one morning a panel truck with two large loudspeakers on top appeared at our front curb. The driver shouted communist propaganda for about five minutes and then departed. My parents thought this was a temporary entity and therefore paid no attention to the same and did nothing.

The following day the same vehicle and driver appeared. This time the verbiage and propaganda continued for twenty minutes, following which my mother called my father and my father called the chief of police in Cuyahoga Falls. My father was told by the chief that the broadcaster was functioning under free speech and nothing could be done. On the third day the same vehicle and individual appeared, and this time the tirade went on for half an hour. My mother was visibly upset and once again called my dad. My father in turn called the labor union director, a good friend of my father since my dad had very recently built the Union Labor Temple in Akron, and we as a family were closely associated with the unions. The union boss said he would take care of the matter. Two days later the van was found burned to a crisp in an alley in Akron, and three days later the driver of the van was found floating down the polluted Cuyahoga River in Ohio, with his hands and feet tied (and he wasn't doing the backstroke). The most impressive aspect of the entire scenario to myself as a child was the complete lack of any concern by my parents about the demise of the driver. I soon learned that I should not feel bad when bad things happen to bad people, and thus the 11th Commandment was born: "Thou shalt not feel bad when bad things happen to bad people."

Chapter 2

As a family we were not permitted to eat refined white sugar, so of course I craved chocolate. I was once able to obtain twenty cents, and thereby bought four Milky Way bars and consumed the same in rapid succession, resulting in one very sick young boy. I had truly learned a lesson.

Perhaps one of the most unfortunate experiences of my life occurred at age eight. Apparently my mother had been told by a nun at the grade school that something had occurred with me, the nature of which I do not recall but which I am sure was not in any way to commend me on my exemplary behavior. It was a decision of my mother to implement austere punishment. In those days my father used a straight razor to shave and sharpen the same with a razor strap. My punishment, therefore, was to take my clothes off and stand in the bathtub, where I received a severe beating in accordance with Amish punishment traditions. I do remember that with each razor strap stroke of one side, my opposite leg would go higher and higher, and although the experience was most unfortunate, I did appreciate that with the leg maneuvers I was learning to dance. In all probability, the rationale came from Proverbs 20:30, "Blows and wounds cleanse away evil, and beatings purge the inmost being." Believe me, my evil was purged, whatever it was that I still do not recall. The rationale for the inflection was simply not known to me.

The punishment resulted in large welts on my back, arms, and legs, and therefore, even though it was warm weather, I wore long-sleeve shirts and pants for a period of three weeks until all the wounds and swelling had subsided. Is it any wonder that I had no affection for my mother thereafter?

My father was an Amish offshoot and professionally an architect. He not only built homes and factories for the underworld, but also built all the Amish schoolhouses in Ohio plus any structure that would require a building permit. It is a rigid philosophy of the Amish that we as humans judge no human being; therefore, evil was not perceived in the underworld by my father.

Around the year 1936 there was a severe polio epidemic in Ohio, and the Amish children were highly afflicted since they had not been vaccinated against polio. There was in essence no way to transport the Amish children back and forth to and from the Children's Hospital in Akron, so my dad put together a group of the mafia men, who then bought a van to transport the children. Therefore, my father was deeply loved by the Amish community.

There was a time when the Amish would not resist thievery, and this became very problematic in Ohio. In conjunction with the underworld and mafia, my dad set up a system to solve the problem. The solution was not difficult to implement, since the thieves were so overt in their crimes, so targeting the specific individuals was easy and resolution of the problem was most definitive (God rest their souls).

At the age of nine my life totally changed after I walked one mile to the movie theater in downtown Cuyahoga Falls. During the western feature I just didn't feel right, and upon completion of the movie I tried to walk home, my heart beating rapidly and my feet, ankles, and knees gradually swelling, until about midpoint when I could not walk and therefore crawled on my hands and knees. Since I had on short pants, it wasn't long before my hands and knees were quite bloodied, and I gave up the task and rolled over on the grass between the sidewalk and the street. A kind lady stopped, actually picked me up, put me in her car, and took me home. Subsequently I found out she was the wife of a union boss whom my father knew. Actually, my father knew all the union bosses, since he had designed and supervised the construction of the Union Labor Temple of Akron, Ohio.

I was in St. Thomas Hospital in Akron for about three weeks, being seen by multiple specialists, including cardiologists, and the ultimate diagnosis was rheumatic fever with severe cardiac involvement and massive congestive heart failure. None of the specialists had seen this problem in a child to this degree before. I was ultimately transported to a pediatric hospital in Cleveland. Bear in mind that this was before the time of antibiotics, and even penicillin was not available. I was seen in consultation by Dr. William Champion, the chief pediatric cardiologist at University Hospitals in Cleveland. I was told later that my parents and my Aunt Kitty were told at that time that my prognosis was zero and that if I did recover from the acute episode that I would be dead by age fifteen. Since my parents were not able to take care of me, I was transferred to the Rainbow Pediatric Hospital in South Euclid, Ohio for the purpose of dying. However, it appeared the Lord had other plans for me. Although I continued in bed, lying flat for twelve months, I gradually progressed and walked out of the hospital fourteen months after admission. I well remember lying flat in bed for twelve months and trying to eat plus entertain myself, and the only therapy that I received during that period of time was eating cow heart twice a week (truly voodoo medicine). It was truly a great relief to be able to at least sit up after that twelve-month period of time, and then gradually learn to walk over the next two months with a walker or crutches.

I ultimately learned that the covering of the heart was swollen (pericarditis) and that the valves were infected (a disaster without antibiotics). I was at high risk for death from infection, and had to be in the room by myself so as not to pick up any additional infection. So what was it like to spend twelve months lying down in a solitary confinement atmosphere? The room was small and consisted of my hospital-type pediatric bed, a nightstand, and a small metal chair with a cushion. The walls were yellow with a large Y-shaped crack which widened in the wintertime and narrowed in the summer with higher humidity. There were no pictures on the walls, and for entertainment I played checkers with myself and occasionally with the janitor who was allowed to come in the room. I had a deck of cards and learned many card tricks, plus I also had a Slinky which I wore out. Was it any wonder I became depressed and cried a lot? There was a witch nurse named Miss Lafond who would chastise me for crying and call me a baby, and I must admit she appeared to be much like Nurse Ratched in the film *One Flew Over the Cuckoo's Nest*.

My entertainment salvation was an old rickety radio with an antenna wire that went up to the curtain rod after having traversed several hooks in the wall. The radio was bulky and hard to tune. However, one day Jimmy Lee (a friend of the family and a key figure in the underworld) appeared at the door with a large box, which he opened and presented to me a wonderful portable radio with its own antenna. Jimmy smiled as I put in the batteries and plugged in the cord. That was actually the rebirth of my entire existence, which I well remember to this day. I listened to soap operas and all the sports events, including the Cleveland Indians baseball team, who at that time had Bob Feller as their star pitcher and Lou Boudreau at shortstop. However, my favorite radio program, sponsored by Ralston-Purina Cereal, was the western with Tom Mix called *Tom Mix Ralston Straight Shooters.*

About six months after receiving my gift I was told that a famous cowboy would be visiting the hospital, as he was giving a major show in Cleveland. It was Gene Autry, and he appeared at my door in western garb with two pearl-handled pistols, and he asked me how long I had been in my bed in that room. When I stated that I had been there for eight months, he told the tour guide to come back in twenty minutes, then came in, sat on the metal chair, and spent thirty minutes playing checkers with me and discussing various items including, "What is your favorite radio program?"

Although I initially did not render accolades to his daily program, I quickly stated, "Tom Mix," where upon Mr. Autry paused for a moment and then told me that Tom Mix had been killed in an auto accident in Arizona about six weeks prior. I had wondered why I had not been able to get Tom Mix's recent programs. I was wise enough, however, to state to Mr. Autry that I truly enjoyed his radio program, particularly the song, "Back in the Saddle Again." When Gene Autry eventually left my room, he invited me to visit him in Hollywood, but I never made it.

When I eventually was allowed out of isolation, I was ten years old and allowed to sit and begin walking, which again took a series of walkers and quad canes and then, finally, no support. I was eventually discharged from the hospital and allowed to go home, since I had not died. The physicians involved could not believe that I had recovered, and the entire recovery and rehabilitation was classified as "a miracle."

In July of 1940 I was only a few months out of my fourteen-month confinement at Rainbow Hospital in Cleveland for rheumatic heart disease and cardiac failure. I had been given a bicycle for rehabilitation and was making good use of it when on the evening of July 31st I was in the drugstore in downtown Cuyahoga Falls picking up some medicine for my mom. A man came running into the store, shouting that there had been a Doodlebug accident at the junction of Front Street and Hudson Drive.

So what was the Doodlebug? It was the Pennsylvania Railroad's gasoline powered single engine car commuter between Akron and Hudson, Ohio, with Hudson being the Pennsylvania Railroad's mainline.

The yellow and white Cuyahoga Falls fire engines had gone out only a few minutes before I entered the drugstore, and with the alarming news I forgot the pills and jumped on my bicycle to ride the one-mile trek down Front Street to the alleged site of the crash. I saw the huge plume of black smoke as I neared the site, but I was not mentally prepared for what I saw. My arrival was probably forty-five minutes after the accident, and the firemen were still extinguishing the flames after the 350 gallons of gasoline had exploded and showered the interior of the Doodlebug, producing a giant fireball.

The Doodlebug's crew of three, the engineer, the conductor, and brakeman, had seen the freight train barreling down toward them on the single track, and they jumped to survive. The freight train was a doubleheader pulling seventy-three cars and no stopping or slowing was feasible.

The freight train telescoped about twelve feet into the Doodlebug, igniting the fuel. Most of the Doodlebug's occupants were propelled to the front and piled up like cooked sausages in a can. The coroner eventually reported that nine of the victims were killed on impact and the remainder was cremated.

So what did I see? As I arrived at the scene, three ambulances from Bellows Ambulance Service in Akron had just arrived and were waiting for the final smoldering mass to be watered down. The most memorable aspect for me was the stench in the air from the forty-three burning bodies, and to this day I get a tidbit of that residual in my brain by just thinking about the situation.

Next on the scene were four engines from the Akron Fire Department, the last of which was an old timer with running boards on the side and a siren that sounded like a sick cow. This was actually the vehicle that carried the heavy extraction equipment utilized subsequently by the firemen. The Akron firemen got off their engines and then just stood there motionless, as much as to think or say, what the hell do we do next.

The first job was to open the large door at the front of the Doodlebug, and this was done with the various tools that had arrived on the sick cow engine. Several of the windows toward the rear of the Doodlebug were still intact and a few bodies could be seen still sitting in their seats in the upright position, fried to a crisp. It was years later in medical school when I ultimately learned that the people had all died instantly instead of being cooked.

All the firemen had a short meeting to determine how to remove the corpses. The heat of the explosion was so intense that it had fused the plastic of the seats to many of the bodies, and the firemen used chainsaws for the separation of not only the seats but also the bodies from each other. Since very little of the inside of the Doodlebug was flammable, the combination of heat and fire was of short duration but devastating.

A crowd was beginning to form, but I was able to stay in front of the pack. The firemen decided to use a two-man cross hand carry to get the corpses from the Doodlebug to the waiting ambulances and vehicles to be conveyed to funeral homes. I remember one corpse which was very well cooked and still in the sitting position as the firemen were removing him from the Doodlebug. The guy was not only sitting but his head was bent forward, as if he was reading at the time of the impact. One of the firemen's boots slipped on the rock bed, jarring the corpse, and in the process the head of the corpse fell off and rolled into the ditch. I was only about one hundred feet away and it was quite a shock, particularly to a ten-year-old kid who was still numb from his own previous two-year health scare.

I stayed until dark and then headed home with unbelievable stories to tell my parents, and they were literally overwhelmed by the scenario which I revealed.

So how did this mess possibly happen? Reports confirm that the engineer on the Doodlebug was told to take a siding at Silver Lake and let the freight go by. Being a survivor of the crash, he said that he never got the message, and ultimately there was no hope of stopping either train, as the Doodlebug was going close to sixty mph and the freight train was a doubleheader. The impact was so profound that the Doodlebug was dragged about a half block down the track yet stayed on the track, but I really doubt if anything would have been different even if the Doodlebug had been knocked off of the track by the impact.

This was one of the most devastating experiences of my life, particularly as a child. I had chosen, until the present, not to discuss the incident hoping that the images would go away—but they have not. The actual memories of the disaster were probably muted by the Second World War, which began less than a year and a half afterwards, and it wasn't until 2005 when three thirteen-year-old middle school students, on the sixty-fifth anniversary of the disaster, decided to raise funds and campaign for a permanent memorial, which they successfully accomplished. Since the Doodlebug disaster was the single highest loss of life of any railroad accident in America, the memory should certainly not be muted.

Finally being home after my hospital confinement was not very enjoyable in that I had missed one and a half years of school and therefore had been put back one year. This was not a serious problem, since I started school at age five, but needless to say it was a considerable adjustment. I had to make new friends, and I found this to be very difficult at first. However, it soon became apparent that I had leadership skills that were recognized by my classmates. I carefully and diabolically put together a group which was called "The Big Five," out of which I was the leader.

By the eighth grade The Big Five was a formidable force, and one day the principal of St. Joseph's grade school, Sister Marie Pierre of the Sisters of Charity of St. Augustine, took me aside. Even though she was one tough bird, I really admired her guts. Sister Pierre told me that a group of boys known as the Morgan Gang was preventing the McNally twins from being able to get to the St. Joseph Catholic School, and she told me definitively to "do something about it." I thought about the mechanics and logistics of the problem and set up a plan. I knew that the Morgan Gang used an abandoned gas station across State Road as their headquarters. I therefore approached a neighbor who was a pyrogenic nut and who had been seriously injured in an explosion. Together we designed a smoke bomb, and Bill, one of the other Big Five members, offered to help deliver the message. One evening we rode our bicycles to the abandoned gas station when nobody was around. The place was totally empty, and we found an unlocked window in the back. I lit the smoke bomb and threw it into the room. Much to my surprise, the smoke bomb apparently ignited a very dusty environment, and in minutes the abandoned gas station was up in flames. Since the Morgan guys were bigger than my gang, and much stronger, we had only one chance to scare the hell out of them and clear out, leaving no room for retaliation.

Bill and I were amazed at how rapidly the abandoned gas station literally exploded in flames. We rode our bikes about a block away to watch the events that transpired. I must admit I was both overjoyed and a bit scared at the time as we observed the yellow and white fire engines from Cuyahoga Falls arriving. In actuality the fire was put out rapidly but the building was totally destroyed. The offshoot was that the McNally twins returned to St. Joseph's grade school unimpeded, and the Morgan Gang could not be found. It just so happened that the father of the Morgan kids was the head of the Communist Party in Akron, and he was removed from the city by the unions, who did not give him an alternative offer. The elimination of the Morgans gave me a false sense of power, and a similar perception spread throughout the youth of my age in

Cuyahoga Falls and North Akron. Fire Chief Seiler, who was my neighbor, somehow caught on that I was involved and called me over to his house. He informed me that I was not Robin Hood and that I should keep my nose clean. I was very careful to follow his advice.

Chapter 3

By the time I was twelve years old the country was hip deep in World War II, and my family had five members in the military. My father was busy building war equipment factories, and my cousin (also my godfather) was a bombardier on a B-29 bomber over Japan. The bombing missions were deadly accurate because of the newly developed Norden bombsight, which helped determine the exact moment bombs were to be released to reach their targets.

A memorable tragedy occurred in my eighth grade year when several of the members of the Big Five were playing Frisbee at the Cuyahoga Falls Gorge. I threw the Frisbee, which was caught by Eugene, who went up in the air to catch it and went off the cliff to his death. It took me years to get over that episode.

As an interjection of humor, the Catholic Church was still entrenched at that time in the confessional, and considering it was long before the days of Stephen Colbert on the CBS late-night show, we decided to avoid the local priest and go to confession at old St. Bernard's Church in downtown Akron. Three of us proceeded by bus to the destination, and it just so happened that the very old pastor was in the confessional that day. Bill tried to confess something in a whisper and the partially deaf elderly pastor blurted out in a loud voice, "You say you committed adultery?" Well, Bill shot out of the confessional of that church and out of Akron in a matter of minutes. We really had no intention of changing our behavior anyway.

To give you more familiarity with the time frame, I will point out that in the year 1943, when I was thirteen years old and living in the state of Ohio, state troopers could not be married and lived in barracks in Cuyahoga Falls and other select locations around the state. World War II was in full tilt and General Patton had recently beaten German General Rommel in North Africa, resulting in thousands of prisoners of war being sent to the United States. America was having a disaster with supply ships (called Liberty ships) going to Europe because of German submarines. Germany was notified that the ships coming to America would have German prisoners of war on them, and this resulted in none of those ships being torpedoed and sunk. It was right about this time that sonar was developed, which in essence was the end of the German U-boats. At the beginning of the war, the German Submarine Corps consisted of thirty-two thousand members, twenty-eight thousand of which ultimately never returned home.

There was a county farm three miles from my home with six German prisoners of war living and working in that facility. I got a job at that farm working in the fields, since the prisoners took care of the animals. One of the most startling things for me to see was that only two of the prisoners had shoes, and those shoes had no soles or heels. The remaining four prisoners had rags wrapped around their feet to function allegedly as shoes. My mother contacted multiple people in our church and obtained many old worn-out boots. She then took the boots to a cobbler in Akron, who took the pieces and put together six pairs of boots, which I thought was a miraculous job. I must say that the German prisoners were more than thankful, and although I spoke no German, we certainly had an excellent relationship.

Relative to speaking German, I wish to point out that when my present wife was six years old, she was sent home from school in the first grade to learn to speak English, as the only language she knew was German.

My farm experiences were unique, such as the time that I installed a belt on a manure spreader but unknowingly put it on backwards. That resulted in a shower of manure upon myself as I attempted to proceed forward. Perhaps the story of stories was my learning to drive. I was only fourteen years of age, and you had to be sixteen in Ohio at that time for a driver's license. The farm boss came over one morning and told me to take the garbage to the dump in the old Mack dump truck. After I explained to him that I did not know how to drive, he told me that now was the time to learn, and he got in his car and left the premises. Well, the events that followed were something to behold. I knew nothing about a single clutch, or particularly the double clutches which were on the old Mack dump trucks. I was no match for the double clutch, as the truck shook forward and backward and from side to side, with the moist garbage shifting with each maneuver and even coming forward over the cab shield, dripping down the windshield. The one German soldier laughed so hard that he was lying on the ground, holding his stomach, and I was later told that he wet his pants. I ultimately was able to learn the double clutch system with one of the prisoners showing me how it was done. He accompanied me in the vehicle over a county road to the dump. Believe me, this was a miraculous accomplishment.

In the summer of 1944 I was fourteen years old and the war was in full tilt. I therefore was able to get a job at Goodyear Aircraft in Akron making Vought Corsair fighter planes. I worked on wing assembly with a woman from Eastern Europe whom I could not understand, and she was very demanding. I had to get up at 5:00 in the morning and take three buses to get to work by 7:00. I then worked twelve hours, took three more buses home, and ultimately landed back home by 9:00 P.M. After three weeks I was so tired that I couldn't do the job, so I had to make a transition. Nevertheless, at the aircraft factory a plane was completed every eight minutes and the slogan was, "Put the Axis behind the eight ball." I ultimately saw a report stating that thirteen thousand total planes were made, and knew that at least I had made an effort.

I quit that employment and went to work at the O'Connor Lumber Company in Akron, owned by my father's best friend. We made bullet seal gas tanks for B-29 bombers and wing floats for Navy PBY recovery planes. I took great pride in putting fancy decorations on these float pontoons until one day we were told to go to all black. It wasn't until after the war that I learned that at nighttime the spotlights from Japanese ships and submarines could illuminate the painted aircraft, but when they were all black the searchlights could not identify the entity in the sky. Therefore, the PBYs would literally camp over the Japanese vessels and drop bombs, a tactic that ultimately was a major factor in the destruction of the Japanese Navy.

Also at age fourteen I would occasionally visit my cousin in Cleveland, and I can remember on weekends going to visit gangster vehicles after car bombings. By the time we got there the bodies were gone, but the pools of blood that remained were impressive. I can remember my Aunt Kitty talking to one of the underworld figures and stating that, "It's too bad about all that car bombing," and the response was, "They were not good people." (I guess it pays to know who the good people are.) Speaking of Aunt Kitty, she drove tractors on the farm, and in essence she drove a car just like a tractor. This means that she would lock the accelerator in high (this could be done with a switch on some of the older cars) and control the speed by releasing the clutch. I must admit that she went through more clutches than rolls of toilet paper and never learned the normal system of driving a car.

As I mentioned before, I would visit my eighteen-year-old cousin Jack periodically on weekends to get away from my boring home. Prior to one weekend he explained to me that he had a meeting planned with his competitor, as both Jack and his competitor were dividing up the territory for selling cigarettes to minors. Jack was a bit nervous about this upcoming meeting and asked me to join him. I really did not think the situation through intelligently, so I joined him at the meeting with his competitor at a pavilion in the local park. The competitor was more aggressive than I anticipated, and when he presented a pistol to substantiate his negotiation point, I stepped up and said that I had in my pocket a plan that would satisfy both parties, upon which I pulled out a snub-nose 22-caliber pistol and fired two shots. The first bullet hit the wall (I was a lousy shot), and the second hit the guy in the left shoulder, and blood flew through his T-shirt and all over the place. His support team disappeared like flies. The wounded competitor was screaming and yelling, and in a car driving by with the windows down a guy heard the turmoil, saw the mess, and proceeded to the next telephone booth to call the authorities. There were no cell phones in those days.

The chain of events that followed was intriguing in that I was temporarily in the Cleveland Heights jail. The charges were shooting an individual plus the illegal possession of a weapon. My relatives rapidly became involved in the whole process, and because of their political influence I was out of jail and on bail in no time. The shooting charge was dropped since the competitor did have a weapon, and therefore my attorney claimed self-defense. However, the issue of possessing an illegal weapon was indefensible, and so rather than face the local consequences, my relatives negotiated with the Cuyahoga County attorney, and arrangements were made for me to be sent to a "far away school." I ended up at a Jesuit boarding school for boys in Prairie Du Chien, Wisconsin that they called Campion.

Two weeks later, before being sent away, I was coming out of Nichols Bakery on State Road in Cuyahoga Falls when an arriving vehicle reported that a big accident had occurred on State Road near Steele's Corners, which was only two miles away. So I hopped on my bike and raced at breakneck speed to the scene, getting there even before the ambulance from Cuyahoga Falls, which had to come from the funeral home. Therefore I was completely uninhibited by either police or an ambulance crew as I went up to the side window of the vehicle which had crashed head-on with a Greyhound bus. The vehicle's driver was draped over the steering wheel and was obviously dead, as the engine had been relocated literally to the front seat. The front seat passenger's head halfway protruded through the windshield, with one bulging eye pointed at me and the other in the opposite direction. I still see that in my mind to this day. In the back seat were two people, one of whom was halfway between the front and back seats and bleeding profusely from the head. The other passenger in the back was as good as dead, as his arms and legs were flailing in the air secondary to an absence of oxygen to the brain. Instead of being disgusted, oppressed or depressed, I had a feeling of exhilaration. This showed me that if I really wanted to be a surgeon, I could do so without fear or anxiety.

Chapter 4

The time had come to fulfill my sentence for my sheer stupidity and attend the Jesuit boarding school for boys in Wisconsin. I packed all that I owned into a large black trunk and took a steam engine train to Chicago, subsequently the Burlington Zephyr from Chicago, and purportedly headed for Minneapolis. However, the train stopped at the campus to let off over one hundred students, as the train track ran along the border of the campus.

The campus itself was quite attractive, with a large beautiful tree in the center. That tree happened to be the subject of the poem "Trees" by Joyce Kilmer, who had attended Campion when it was a college.

I was engineered to Koska Hall, which had to be at least one hundred years old, and up the metal stairs to the second floor, where I was steered to my cubicle. Yes, it was an eight by fourteen-foot cubicle with no top and a curtain door, the contents of which included a rickety bed (also probably one hundred years old), an old low dresser with three drawers and a mirror, and a wardrobe and small chair. I now knew that I was in prison.

I hated the damn place and couldn't figure out why some families actually paid to send their kids there. I soon found out that Campion was the highest academically related high school in the nation, and therefore decided to go for broke to be a success, as I really did not have an alternative. I would aim to touch the stars, and I did.

For all four years I was third in my class of eighty-eight students. Also, hard to believe, I had a perfect conduct record for all four years. I actually thrived on the rigid militaristic discipline of the Jesuits to the degree that some of the guys actually believed me to be nuts (an accurate observation). I only had two disciplinary issues and both were determined to be of self-defense origin and were disregarded. I must add that two upperclassman learned not to pick on a little guy like me.

I also made up my mind to recondition myself physically, since I had not really done so following my rheumatic fever except for the use of a bicycle. This meant that my upper extremities needed a lot of work. I therefore joined a pick-up basketball league and played for one hour after each school day, and it did the trick.

In my second year I shared a nice room with another guy who didn't, for some reason, talk to me, but that's the way it goes. Due to my academic status, I subsequently was allowed a very nice room in an elite dormitory, one in which I occupied for my third and fourth years, giving me at least some element of satisfaction in the overall picture relative to the total environment at Campion.

A few startling events occurred during my time at Campion. Walking one morning with my best friend to the chapel, as we were talking he stopped and fell over dead. I was devastated and actually mad at God. The issue was unsettled for years both with me and the boy's family.

After my second year at Campion, I was home in the summer helping my dad do surveying for building. I was in his office when a guy came in and announced that he had a new excavating company in Akron and expected my dad to give him some work. Dad explained to the man that he had used DeBartolo Excavating for many years and had no reason to make the change. Dad then had two threatening calls from this guy, the second being quite austere. Subsequently Dad met with two of the union bosses, seeking advice. The bosses told Dad that they would take care of the problem, and two days later the offender received a Christmas present of thirteen slugs in the back, and I don't mean for fishing.

My parents had no remorse of this outcome, thus the 11th Commandment again took effect. Dad continued to use DeBartolo Excavating, and three years later I drove by a lot outside of Akron where the offender's excavating equipment lay resting and rusting, as the Amalgamated Rubber Workers of America had chosen to neither seize nor sell the inert machinery.

After the second year at Campion, the war had ended and construction shifted from military needs to civilian needs. I wanted and needed a summer job, since I had to pay a sizable portion of the tuition at Campion as part of my punishment. At age fifteen it was not easy to get a job, and union membership was necessary for most real paying jobs in the greater Akron area, especially since I was seeking work for only a three-month period of time. However, through my dad and the Hod Carriers Union I joined both the AFL and CIO unions before their merger in 1955. I then proceeded to work as a hod carrier, serving bricklayers and being constantly slowed down by the union boys. We were supposed to take our time in building the Richardson School in Cuyahoga Falls, Ohio, and I was working too fast.

As stated previously, in my third year at Campion I was in the classic and good boy dormitory, which had spacious rooms, and mine faced the golf course and Burlington Railroad track. I enjoyed seeing the Burlington Zephyr and the Empire Builder go by each day, with the former headed for the Twin Cities and the latter on to Seattle. My floor monitor, Father Bachhuber, was a very kind Jesuit with a mousy-type personality. Being diabolical and a master of deceit, I did pull a fast one on him. I had a radio; however, this radio required an extensive aerial since we were nowhere near a high power radio station. I had a long wire which extended from the radio and along the floor and then connected through an adapter at the door jamb. The effect was such that if you opened the door, the radio could be on but the aerial would disconnect and the radio would suddenly be silent. Occasionally I would play the radio after allowed hours, and Father Bachhuber would sneak down the hall in his soft shoes and throw the door open. Of course the adapter would separate and the radio would be silent. He would be totally unable to figure out what was going on. I would then secondarily step on another adapter at my foot, so that when he would open and shut the door nothing would happen. This scenario continued on several occasions. Father ultimately stated that "the devil is involved," and how right he was.

I continued my endless study habits, beating everybody in the class except two guys. The number one fellow, Bill Sullivan, became a very prominent Jesuit and president of Seattle University, so I guess I shouldn't feel too bad. Campion continued to be one of the most scholastically accomplished high schools in the nation, so that's what can be achieved with four years of marine-type discipline and confinement. Oh yes, we were confined to the campus. Subsequent studies revealed that two-thirds of the class attained ultimate professional status, so the effort was truly worthwhile.

By the way, when I entered Campion at age fourteen, I still had a slight southern accent from the days with my black mammy. After hearing my voice on the tape recorder, I was coached vigorously to learn to speak without an accent, which resulted in my forceful voice even to this day, very unusual for an eighty-seven-year-old male. It is interesting to note that the last phrase of southern lingo that I had to discard was the word "safanoon," which translated means "this afternoon."

I have frequently been asked whether or not I ever had any fun during my time at Campion, and the response is that I loved racing, particularly air races, and I attended the air races in Cleveland every year. I was about sixteen years old and present at the races in Cleveland when jets were being used for the first time in closed course racing. Well, it did not work out in that the stress of the rapid turns popped the rivets on the wings, so back they went to prop planes for closed course racing. However, my life with air racing ended when my hero, Bill Odom, crashed into a home in Berea, Ohio, which in turn actually ended the air races in Cleveland.

During the first couple years that I was at Campion, the war was still on and I had a fanatic compulsion to go to West Point to be a fighter pilot. This was before the days of the Air Force being formed as a military unit. I had significant knowledge of aircraft and a driving compulsion to fulfill that need. However, the war ended and I had to decide into which direction I would proceed, and medicine appeared to be the most workable career for my personality. I subsequently received a scholarship from Campion to John Carroll University in Cleveland, another Jesuit institution. This was right about the time that the Korean War started, and the students at John Carroll were studying frantically so as not to be drafted, and I was not the exception.

We had a sizable unit of navy personnel in the science classes, and we were at a definite disadvantage as nonmilitary individuals. The navy guys would sit their smartest officer next to a pipe at examination time, and he would tap out the correct answers on the pipe in Morse code. The navy guys always got the best grades.

One of my summer jobs while at John Carroll was testing race cars for Firestone Tire and Rubber Company in Akron, again obtaining the job through the unions. I suppose you think it is glamorous and exciting to test race cars. Well, it was... for about three days. I soon got incredibly bored, as the track was quite confined and there was a governor on the engine set at 120 mph. The only real entertainment that I had was learning to skip or jump gears on the gear shift slot and yet not strip the gears in the process. How is that for excitement? We only worked about three hours a day anyway at the race track, so I was able to get additional work to supplement the income.

After my first year at John Carroll my old pediatrician from the days when I had rheumatic fever, Dr. Pittinger, was the coroner for Summit County, which included Akron. I asked him if I could help with some of the autopsies, as I was interested in being a forensic pathologist (just like the present day Dr.Ducky on *NCIS*). Well, it was a marvelous experience. Since I was home on weekends and the best accidents occurred on the weekends, I received a tremendous education. I even remember the names of some of the victims, particularly a sixteen-year-old boy with the initials of JHL who was riding his new motorcycle at high speed and hit a pickup truck head-on. I remember lifting his head at the St. Thomas Hospital morgue. His skull felt like a bowl of Jell-O. I then carefully moved his head to the side and it rendered the sound of falling marbles. Thus I was learning lessons that would carry me into the future and help set my pace on the road of life and medicine. I soon learned that if you can't stand the heat, get out of the furnace.

Chapter 5

One of the most memorable experiences at John Carroll University was meeting Angelo Milano at a party in West Hill in Akron, Ohio. Angelo was the nephew of the Milano brothers, a Cleveland underworld family, and was in America for one year to attend John Carroll University. He became my mechanism of transport back to school on Sunday evenings in his Alpha Romeo, and I had never seen such a car like that before. I would carry my book bag and laundry bag the one-half mile up Chestnut Boulevard to State Road, where he would pick me up. I would explain to him American words and slang as he would give me phrases in Italian. I could easily relate, since I had taken four years of Latin at Campion, and we had lots of laughs in the exchange. However, we never discussed his family or the underworld.

My older sister was a nun at the time who taught some of his family and the Yankovic kids (whose family included "Frankie" Yankovic, known as "America's Polka King") at Jesu School, which was right across the street from John Carroll University. She actually kept in touch with many of those families for many years, and to this day, in her confinement, those are still some of her closest friends outside of the convent.

Speaking of Frankie Yankovic, it was through him that I was introduced to stand-up comedy for weddings and celebrations in the greater Cleveland area, and this was a mechanism by which I made enough money to pay my way through college, with a little help. One of the bands that I truly enjoyed was the Chardon Polka Band. To this day my sister, the ninety-year-old nun, lives in a convent in Chardon, Ohio. By the way, Chardon was the home of several of the key mafia bosses—truly a religious community. There was also a young female Polish polka band that sang in Polish, and I can't spell the title of the band or their individual names, but they were real chicks. I truly enjoyed listening to and watching their antics.

So what did I do at John Carroll University? Well, I studied my ass off, as I was fanatic and compulsive in reaching my goal of medical school. In the three years that I was at JCU, I got all A's except one B in physics and a C in theology (I did not agree with the teacher). After three years I applied to three medical schools: St. Louis University; Marquette in Wisconsin; and Loyola in Chicago. I was accepted at all three. I approached the dean at John Carroll and asked for a degree after finishing two years of medical school, as that was a procedure seen at other institutions. However, the request was vehemently denied. I finally received the degree from John Carroll University five years ago, at the age of eighty-two. So do you think they may have been ruminating for some money?

I was frequently asked over the years, "What happened to Campion?" Well, in 1995 Campion became the Wisconsin State Juvenile Corrections Center, and a few years later it became the Wisconsin State Adult Medium Security Penitentiary. So in reality, nothing changed at all.

So which of the three medical schools did I choose? Well, I chose Loyola of Chicago, since I felt there would be a larger indigent clinical base for learning, and I was correct. So hold onto your hats, because off we go on the venture.

The old Loyola Medical School in Chicago was the rickety old structure at 706 South Walcott Ave., in the heart of the slums and across the street from the old Cook County Hospital. The medical school was a magnificent structure from another century. Cook County Hospital was so close that you could walk out the front door of the medical school and walk right into the emergency department of the Cook County Hospital. I will elaborate on this point later.

I had been a top student in high school and college before hitting medical school, but I soon met my match. I had to study twice as hard as the others to make the grade. In the first year you are given a cadaver (dead body) to dissect. There were four of us to each cadaver, and we named our cadaver "Ernest." We hung a sign overhead stating, "Working in dead Ernest."

The first year was brutal, but physiology (how the body works) confirmed my belief in a God, as I could not believe how one person could keep alive for one minute. Therefore, medicine and science introduced me to and confirmed my impression of a higher power.

There was no free time during that first year, and for an occasional reprieve we would eat at a restaurant around the corner from the medical school called the Greeks. Believe me when I say that was quite a cross-section of humanity, with doctors and medical personnel from all over the world. Actually I fit into the picture very well, and one evening, after a couple beers, I even entertained the crowd with a little dance on the large table to my favorite song on the jukebox. Even the owner was entertained with the antics. However, that was only a one-time venture.

During my first year I met a couple of classmates whose fathers were key figures in Chicago, and I cashed in on the connections. In a subsequent segment I will tell about my friend whose father owned the Blue Note Café on Michigan Avenue, which gave me the opportunity to meet Les Paul and Mary Ford, truly an enjoyable experience.

However, the two key guys in my life were Wally and Jim. Jim's father was the fire prevention chief in Chicago, and therefore on certain occasions I rode around in his limo with great gusto. Yet Wally was my key contact, so let me tell you a few of the stories.

Wally's father was a police captain in the plainclothes unit of the precinct near the medical school. I expressed to him my interest in forensic medicine and asked to accompany one of his weekend tours, not knowing what might happen. He consented, and on my first weekend with the unit they were investigating a murder of a professor from the University of Chicago. We went through much paperwork and came to no definitive conclusions except that the professor was obviously killed by a strong male. There was one more person to be questioned and it was the professor's girlfriend Missy. So off we went to interview Missy at her apartment. I well remember that Missy was not only good looking but she had gorgeous legs. The interview lasted about a half an hour and I don't remember much of the content, but after we returned to the precinct headquarters I mentioned that Missy had larger bases of the hair stubs on her shaved legs than usually seen on a female. The sergeant raised his eyes. I then mentioned that Missy held her cigarette like a male and smelled like a male. The captain jumped up and corralled the unit, which immediately went back to visit Missy in her apartment. This time they caught her in her underwear, and the evidence was obvious—they had their man. I was famous for three weeks at the precinct.

However, the incident that I see to this day centered around our eating lunch at a lunch counter on the near North Side, and subsequently getting up to pay our respective bills at the cash register. Luke, who was a cop, was standing behind the guy paying his bill, and I was behind Luke. The guy pulled out a gun and pointed it at the cashier, demanding the cash. Luke paused a moment then presented his pistol, pointing it straight at the guy, who did not follow the command to freeze. Subsequently he turned his body and pistol toward Luke, who fired off two quick shots, one of which took off the back of the guy's head. I was dumbfounded and froze. The now dead guy's accomplice ran out the door to an awaiting vehicle. One of the other cops in our group rapidly followed close behind and fired two shots at the tires of the fleeing vehicle, miraculously hitting one, which resulted in the car rimming down the street and right into the loving arms of another police vehicle which just happened to be in the area. I did not go outside and missed the show, but instead stayed inside, helping the cashier clean the pieces of brain out from between the protruding keys of the cash register. She was weeping, and I admit that after a few moments of assisting I was also crying profusely, following which we all drove to the precinct headquarters in silence. To this day I still see the little black lady weeping as we cleaned that cash register, and it took great effort to keep my tears from falling into the pieces of the brain that were still scattered about.

I had two more allotted weekends to spend at the precinct, and this was before Commissioner White cleaned up the Chicago Police Department and implemented new rigid rules. However, I was able to sneak in one more safari. I had heard of the great cop Frank Pape, who was famous for killing cop killers; he was known for never bringing a cop killer back alive. I thought, *what a great way to go out*, and much to my surprise, Detective Pape agreed to take me on for the two weekends. He was amused at my youthful appearance and teased me profusely, but his cardinal blow was when he placed the following sticker on the windshield of my old 1937 Ford: "If this abandoned and disabled vehicle is not removed within 24 hours, it shall be towed." Since I was allowed to park in the precinct's parking area, the entire contingent of police thought this was a very humorous maneuver, laughing the most when I tried to scrape the well-glued message off the windshield.

The first weekend with Pape was dull, as we made a few runs that did not materialize. The second week I watched him put on his bulletproof vest (which I also had to wear), then place a glass plate inside the front of his vest. I asked him, "What's that for?" He told me to wait and I would see.

We drove to a four-story abandoned warehouse on the south side of Chicago, and when we arrived Frank made no effort to be quiet as he stomped up the decrepit stairway to the fourth floor and flung open a squeaky door. Next, he took out the glass plate from his vest and threw it to the other side of the hall. A guy came running out of the end room and fired two shots at the site where the glass plate had shattered. The guy subsequently turned and ran down the hall into what he thought was another room, not realizing that such was an abandoned elevator shaft. I heard a scream and then a thud, which was followed by Pape turning and walking down the stairs and over toward his car. I asked him if he was going to check the body and he replied, "No, the rats will take care of that."

Chapter 6

In the third and fourth years of medical school we did clinical rotations, which meant the various specialties, and it was not unusual that these would occur seven days a week. However, I did get in one more weekend safari in my fourth year, and I actually got paid. There were two guys in my class, Walt and Tom, who were older veterans from a small town in Pennsylvania. They had a military background and therefore worked routinely on weekends for the North Shore Patrol, a security agency, where they would don uniforms, carry pistols and drive a marked police vehicle.

One weekend they needed additional coverage and asked me if I would cover the American Hose & Rubber Company in Skokie, Illinois for the full weekend, day and night. This was great since that was a do-nothing job with plenty of time to study. All went well until Sunday afternoon, when a sedan pulled up in front of the place and two guys got out. I stood behind the door as the one guy opened it, and immediately rammed the barrel of my pistol into his ribs, demanding to see an ID. He showed me some card and I had no idea what was on it, but I did allow him and his associate to proceed while keeping my hand on the pistol in the holster and staying close behind them through the entire tour of the plant.

While I figured that would be the last weekend at American Hose & Rubber for me, I was pleasantly surprised to discover that the visitor was in fact the owner. He insisted that I be the full-time weekend guard, which was simply not possible. However, I must admit my ego went up a few points just to be asked.

Needless to say, the vast majority of my time was related to my education and training at Loyola Medical School, as that was my primary focus. We were allowed to take major electives in the fourth year, and I chose the Cook County Hospital Emergency Department for one month. I was about to learn what life was all about.

The first week was a lot of routine stuff, but I well remember a guy brought in with literally his guts hanging out. He was a big, fat fellow and believe me, there were a lot of intestines. He had been sliced from stem to stern, and the chief resident physician told me the patient would not survive. The chief resident went over to the patient with a pair of scissors and told me to watch as he started to cut the bowel into pieces with the scissors. The patient demonstrated no pain reaction. The doctor next put down the scissors, picked up a piece of the gut and stretched it between two fingers, causing the patient to scream in pain. Then the resident physician said to me, "See, that is why a leak in the bowel may not be painful but any distention is." I truly learned a lesson as the very heavy patient went on to the next world.

Another large man came in, close to death due to a bucket of gunshot in his belly. The resident physician pushed the man's cart into the corner of the room and told me that it was another one of those "air conditioning jobs." I was learning the terminology of the Chicago underworld.

A large black woman was brought into the emergency department in prolonged labor, and since I had skillfully and purposefully avoided all OB/GYN rotations, I fumbled to console the lady who was becoming more impatient with me. I tried to explain to her the importance of relaxing, and that doing so would help the situation. I also made the mistake of stating, "It's really not that bad," to which she looked at me and fired back, "Hey boy, did you ever shit a watermelon?" Needless to say, I had no answer.

One noon day I was walking with a classmate from the medical school to the emergency department when a patient jumped out of the third story window and landed on his head about ten feet in front of us. Probably for the first time in my life, I was speechless. Needless to say, the patient was dead.

Without question one of the most memorable events that occurred in my lifetime took place in the Cook County Hospital Emergency Department where I was working one evening. A guy was brought in by the police with a bloodied towel around his neck, and the resident physician announced, "Another suicide screw-up." When I asked for an explanation, he took the towel off the patient's neck and said, "See, just a lot of little veins got cut," and he demonstrated to me that this is what happens when the head is bent forward at the time of the slash. He then showed me on himself the maneuver of full extension (holding the head all the way back) and said, "This is what's required to cut the right stuff." While the resident turned and walked away, I witnessed the patient pull out a switchblade, throw his head all the way back, and with a mighty swing of the blade slice open his entire front neck, including all the muscles, blood vessels, and the trachea. The first squirt of blood almost hit the ceiling, the second hit the wall, while the third hit the floor and formed a pool of blood where the body subsequently fell. I heard a couple of gurgles in his trachea, following which his body squirmed and then stopped. I stood there absolutely frozen. The resident physician came over and said, "See, it works." To this day I still envision that scenario.

I also remember an immigrant Puerto Rican family that was brought into the emergency department, extremely ill after having eaten a dead pig that they found in the back of the farmers' market nearby. All six members of the family had acute trichinosis and all six died, including the two and three-year-old children. I must admit I had great sorrow for days afterward. They actually burned up with fever for over two days, and there was no adequate treatment at that point in time.

So was medical school all work and no play? Well, I was quite the extrovert and ended up being the social chairman for our fraternity. My campaign manager had the bulletproof claim that I was the only one eligible for the position of social chairman since I was the only one who had had all the social diseases. Even though I didn't know what all the social diseases were, I accepted the accolade and received the appointment.

A memorable event occurred when I was social chairman in that I had a meeting with my counterpart at Northwestern University Medical School. As we were riding in an elevator one afternoon, my partner was smoking a cigarette. The elevator stopped at one of the floors and the chief of neurosurgery at Northwestern University Medical School, the famous Loyal Davis, got on the elevator, and believe me, nobody smoked in his presence.

So the elevator had stopped on the third floor and on comes Loyal Davis, distastefully sniffing the air. My associate, Thatcher, flipped the cigarette into the corner of the elevator floor as Dr. Davis, continuing to sniff heartedly, then proclaimed, "Thatcher, is that your cigarette?" Pointing to the cigarette which was still emitting smoke, Thatcher quickly responded, "You can have it, Sir, you saw it first." It was a rare moment to see Loyal Davis smile, and he actually did. By the way, Loyal Davis was Nancy Reagan's father.

While I graduated twenty-sixth out of sixty-six students, I obviously was not the brightest. I still looked the youngest, and my classmate and good friend Heinz Weiner was the oldest. He had been a soldier in the Nazi army, and we had many interesting conversations but ultimately both went our separate ways.

Chapter 7

Back in my day, internships were achieved primarily by class standing. Being twenty-sixth in the class and not from a well-known medical school, I was chosen by Old St. Luke's Hospital at 1439 South Michigan Avenue in downtown Chicago as one of their interns. I was not married at the time, so I was living on the thirteenth floor overlooking the Rock Island Railroad Station and Soldiers Field. I decided to be the best intern that St. Luke's had ever had, and have been told that I accomplished that goal.

So what happened? The internship was classified as rotating, but I was able to concentrate on the surgical specialties. However, realizing that internal medicine was critical if one wished to be a successful surgeon, I therefore put great emphasis and time learning as much as I could about the specialty of internal medicine along with the other specialties.

There was an internist by the name of Dr. McMahon who lived about twenty-two miles from the hospital. I spent as much time with him as I could, as he was an excellent teacher, and I learned a tremendous amount about practical internal medicine in the process of being attentive to his instruction. I was literally his personal attendant and told him that if his hospitalized patients needed anything at any time and he was not available, just to have the nurses call me. It just so happened that Dr. McMahon only had to come into the hospital on three occasions in the nine months that I functioned in that capacity.

When I told Dr. McMahon that I dreamed of going into an orthopedic residency training program at Harvard, I stated such in passing. I found out subsequently that he wrote to the dean at the medical school at Harvard and stated that I was the hardest working intern that he had ever seen. To jump a little ahead of the story, when I got to Harvard two years later, Dr. McMahon's brother, Father Tim McMahon (a Catholic priest), was on the Board of the Massachusetts General Hospital, Harvard's teaching facility, and his father was a leading political figure in Boston, which is why I had clear sailing.

However, the backup dynamo at St. Luke's was Dr. Paul Hollinger, chief of otolaryngology at the University of Illinois. He handled his big cases at St. Luke's and literally ended up performing the major cancer surgery for the throat. I subsequently became his right-hand man and first assistant surgeon in surgery, and tended each patient as if it were my family member. On occasion I would even sleep on a cot next to his patients at night to suction them out when they were choking.

During that same time period Dr. Hollinger was developing the Brubaker endoscopic surgical camera, and I would frequently operate the camera during the surgical procedure. Dr. Hollinger also rarely had to come into the hospital on off-hours, as I attended his patients with great care as well. I had also made a few recommendations on the improvement of the Brubaker camera and, to my surprise, they were incorporated in the new model.

To jump ahead again, when I got to Harvard subsequently my boss was Dr. Joseph Barr, Sr., chief of Orthopedics at Harvard and the first man in the world to do disc surgery, for whom I eventually ended up working in his practice until I was drafted into the Vietnam War. Dr. Barr eventually told me that he had received a letter from Dr. Hollinger stating, "If you don't take this kid, I will." In fact, I was all set to go to the University of Illinois and train under Dr. Hollinger when the acceptance from Harvard came during my general surgical residency.

To get back to my days at St. Luke's, I literally worked 24/7 to learn and keep busy. I was not married at the time and one early evening, after being in the building for three weeks without a respite, I decided to walk down Michigan Avenue just to get out of the place. I was not yet directly in front of the Conrad Hilton Hotel when I saw three guys come around the corner and straight toward me, the middle guy wielding a knife. He said to me, "Give me your wallet." As I produced the wallet, I explained that I only made $35 a month (which was true—plus room and four meals a day). As I extended the wallet, I noted a sudden expression of fear on the face of the guy with the knife, and abruptly he and his two accomplices turned around and ran back around the corner of the hotel. I was startled and looked to my right, where the attacker had looked, and I saw a large man dressed in black. I looked to my left and saw the exact same image. As I put the wallet back in my pocket, I turned to thank the guy on the right and he was gone. I turned to the left and that guy was gone. I turned around and ran back to the hospital and up to my room, where I sat on the side of the bed for about an hour, just contemplating. I reached the conclusion that this was miracle number two in my life and the Lord must have something in mind for me. I also decided to keep this situation silent, since I did not feel that anyone would believe me.

I returned to Cleveland for a week of vacation and was out to dinner with my cousin's husband who had been a submarine commander in the Second World War and who, at the time of my visit, was an executive of one of the nation's largest stock brokerage companies in Cleveland. He could not understand why I was not going in to the brokerage business, since there were millions to be made with ease. It wasn't until years later that I realized the mechanism that he was explaining to me was inside trading. Needless to say, I did not choose a stock market career even in my ignorance of what it was.

At that time it was required for one training for a surgical specialty to first take training in general surgery. For me the requirement was designated as one year, and while that year was not terribly exciting, I did get notice that I would be able to do my orthopedic training at Harvard, which certainly fired up my interest and enthusiasm. I actually could not believe it at the time, since I did not know about all the background communication by Dr. McCauley and Dr. Hollinger at St. Luke's with the dean of Harvard Medical School and the chief of the Department of Orthopedics at Harvard/Mass General. It was hard to believe but I gladly accepted.

My general surgical training at St. Francis Hospital in Evanston, Illinois was routine and included a very strict surgeon from the Mayo Clinic named Martin Fahey. He had only one way to do things. That fit in quite well with my compulsive personality, which ultimately reached its culmination later in the U.S. Army. Dr. Martin Fahey had a brother named Dr. J.J. Fahey, a very prominent orthopedic surgeon in the greater Chicago area and who did most of his work at St. Francis. I spent some time with Dr. J.J. Fahey, and he liked my compulsive thoroughness. Without my knowledge he also sent a recommendation to Dr. Joseph Barr, Sr. at Harvard on my behalf. I ultimately learned from Dr. Barr that Dr. J.J. Fahey's note stated, "This guy gets it done and done right."

The highlight of my year at St. Francis occurred when I was getting out of my car one morning in the parking lot of the hospital, and two nurses came running out of the emergency department to grab me. In essence the disaster was that a young woman, eight months pregnant, was the unrestrained front seat passenger in a car involved in a front-end collision, and she had either hit the dashboard or something on it, severely damaging her trachea. A nearby police car adroitly drove her right to the emergency department, where her trachea was closing off. I ran into the ER as she was turning blue and yelled, "Trach set!" and the nurse grabbed a tracheotomy surgical package, the kind of which I had learned to use at Cook County Hospital. At this point the patient was blue. I slashed open the front of her neck and cut a quick hole in the trachea, followed by a rapid insertion of a tracheostomy tube. She gave out a loud gasp as air shot into her lungs, accompanied by a loud whistle. Within a minute all the blue on her face was gone and within a few more minutes she was back to normal white color. The nurse helping me went off to the corner of the room and cried with joy. The other nurse was jumping up and down and screaming. It took me a moment to appreciate the little miracle that had occurred right before our eyes.

At this point Dr. J.J. Fahey was walking by the ER, heard all the turmoil, and came in and asked, "What the hell is going on here?" When told the story he walked over to the patient and said, "Oh my God." He walked away about ten feet, turned around and came back, looked at her a second time and again said, "Oh my God," and a huge smile appeared on his face. Needless to say, I also was very pleased with the outcome.

I hurried off to surgery, since I was now late. The next day, after surgery the head nun administrator asked me to come to the conference room on the first floor, as the patient's parents had flown up from Chicago. When I walked into the room, the girl's mother grabbed me and held me tight, weeping profusely. She wouldn't let go, saying, "You saved my baby and her baby." For the first time the full impact was realized by myself, and I also started to cry uncontrollably. I had never wept so hard before. The head nun did not know what to do, so she ordered milk and cookies be brought up on a cart. When we all regained composure, the mother said, "If it's a boy we will name it David; if it's a girl, we will name it Florence," (that's actually my real name). So somewhere out there is a David or a Florence whom I have never met.

The only other items of interest were my encounters with an Emil Grubbe, the first physician in America to use x-ray without protection and who will be discussed in more detail later in this book. Also, St. Francis Hospital was the Pediatric Burn Center for poor children, and I spent days cleaning wounds with ether before the invention of Silvadene, an antibiotic used to prevent infection in burn patients. I would come home smelling like an anesthesia machine, but it was worth it.

Chapter 8

So it was time for the big step. I was about twenty-seven years old and still looked like I was sixteen. I was headed to the Harvard Orthopedic Program, consisting of Children's Medical Center and the Massachusetts General Hospital, both recently rated number one in the nation by *US News & World Report*.

So what did I find? The atmosphere at the Children's Medical Center was very stern and centered around Dr. William T. Green, the chief and chairman of the department, and the hours were arduous. When one was on call every third weekend, you would end up going to work on a Friday morning and not be home again until Monday evening. I can remember being so tired during some of those weekend call routines that I would go to the back restroom on the third floor next to the skyway to the Dana-Farber Research Institute and sleep on the toilet in the sitting position for twenty minutes.

It was very difficult to please Dr. Green, who actually was a master procrastinator. Dr. David Grice, however, was Dr. Green's associate professor and, although gruff, was very knowledgeable and direct, plus a rapid decision maker. I related more definitively with Dr. Grice, who was my mentor. Sad to say, he was subsequently killed in an air crash in the Boston Harbor when seagulls filled the air intakes on the prop jet Electra. This occurred shortly after he had been appointed chief at the Children's Medical Center in Philadelphia, so I was blessed in having him as my mentor the entire year that I was at Children's in Boston. His loss was certainly tremendous for the entire orthopedic world.

Children's Medical Center in Boston had patients from all over the world, and this introduced me to many new cultures as well as families of celebrities, particularly in the cancer unit. In those days, the Dana-Farber Research Institute was a very prominent attachment to the Children's Medical Center, particularly for bone and soft tissue cancer treatment, which at that time was in its early days.

Relative to general orthopedic care at Children's we were still in the primitive stages, as I spent many useless hours putting plaster casts on the legs and feet of children at the insistence of the parents when this therapy was not only unnecessary but totally useless. Also, practical surgical experience at Children's was rare, so I did not consider that year as a priority. I was still acutely aware that I had graduated twenty-sixth in my class at medical school and was one lucky dog to be there. I did all the pup (grunt) chores with a smile and was determined to be approved. Although I was fearless and brainless, I could still get things done. I worked with enthusiasm, and that was actually recognized.

On I moved to Massachusetts General Hospital, and it was a welcome relief both from the general atmosphere and the attitude of the attending physicians. The procedure was to take three new training residents per year; in this case it was Ed Wyman, John Saville, and myself, David Florence. Six months into the rotation, John Saville went sailing with his brother on Chesapeake Bay and died of a heart attack before reaching shore. When Ed and I found out about this we just looked at each other, knowing that we had just inherited John's workload, which we did gladly.

My skills of getting things done proved to be apparent. In those days there were about five total structures composing the MGH, including the main hospital plus the Baker building and the Phillips House, which we softly renamed the "P house." Today there are approximately thirty buildings composing the complex, including the research facilities.

About eight months into the residency, the chief resident, was scheduled to remove a bone tumor from the upper spine of a patient. To do this, a general surgeon was required to go through the chest and make the exposure. I was scheduled as second assistant to help the full-time general surgeon teacher open up the chest and expose the spine and bone. When I asked the general surgeon if I could start the procedure (Fearless David), he just looked at me. Without thinking, the assistant professor said okay, go ahead, anticipating that I would just do the initial phase with a scalpel. Well, the scalpel flew and the retractors were in place before you could bat an eye. The teaching general surgeon said (with a Boston accent), "Where the hell did you learn to do that?"

I explained that I had worked with a prominent cancer surgeon in my general surgical residency, and the teacher replied that he had never seen anyone coagulate bleeders as rapidly as I did. After I took my surgical mask off, he next asked, "How old are you?" I relayed to him that I was, in fact, twenty-seven years old. In any case, he congratulated me on my surgical skills.

Right about this time all hell broke loose in the Roxbury housing project. I lived in the white people section with my wife and two very young children. When the riots grew and tires were being burned in the streets, the Roxbury police gave me three weeks to get out. Since we were on the first floor and had insecure windows, the police guarded the apartment twenty-four hours a day until we moved to Belmont, which my young daughter appropriately named "Belnut." We moved into the top of a two flat owned by an Italian lady, and subsequently a third child was born. My children spent many hours with Mrs. Calabro and ended up speaking one-third Italian, one-third English, and one-third their own language. It was very confusing, and trying to figure out what they were talking about was a chore.

I took no vacation time at Children's Medical Center or likewise during my entire tour at Massachusetts General Hospital. The time was simply too valuable to waste. With John gone, Ed and I divided the chores and became lifetime friends that ended with Ed dying much too soon. Ed had a neat red convertible and a large black Bernese Mountain dog. When we rode in the convertible with the top down, the dog sat upright in the passenger seat in front and I was relegated to the back seat.

Many interesting and unusual incidents occurred along my journey at MGH, and these are just a few of the lighter points. At the time of my residency a very powerful senator from Massachusetts, Leverett Saltonstall, was very active in Washington, and he had a daughter who was a patient of Dr. Barr, a sturdy woman who dearly loved mules. I also loved mules, so I finally found a soulmate and we developed an ethereal relationship. However, looking at the serious side of the situation, I was blessed to be assigned to the section where Dr. Joseph Barr, Sr. had his patients. He was the first man in the world to do disc surgery, and patients from all over the world came to see him, which was an education in itself for me. Since Dr. Barr's COPD was becoming progressive, I was doing more and more for and with him. Since I had not had a close relationship with my father, guess who filled that role? I was always his first assistant at surgery, and it was not unusual that we would get halfway through the procedure and, even with his oxygen on full tilt, he would tell me to "take over," and he would leave the room. At first the nurses were a bit apprehensive about the situation, but as Dr. Barr's COPD worsened, the nurses felt much more secure with me. I was doing more and more of the surgical procedures, even on patients from other countries who were told by Dr. Barr that I was their doctor and surgeon. My young-appearing face still caused many to pause, but I stepped right up to the plate.

As time went on, I literally took over more and more of Dr. Barr's chores, and upon completion of the residency, joined his group. So the guy who was twenty-sixth in his class in medical school had joined the most prestigious orthopedic practice in America, which consisted of Doctors Ober, Brewster, Barr, Hugenberger, Record, deLorem and Florence. It's not all bad, at times, to be hind tit on the hog.

However, the memories of my training continue, as I recall my neurosurgical experiences under Dr. Richard Sweet, the chief of neurosurgery at Harvard and Massachusetts General Hospital, and also one of the top neurosurgeons in the nation. Dr. Sweet had a very high-pitched voice, and was fascinated with the fact that I could hand him whatever instrument he needed before he verbalized the request. I worked with Dr. Sweet on cervical spine cases but no skull surgery. He was one tough bird, and even fired a resident physician when I was making rounds with him. For once in my life I was momentarily scared, as I did not want to be the Julius LaRosa of Massachusetts General Hospital. (Remember Arthur Godfrey?) Ultimately, though, my experiences with Dr. Sweet were excellent.

Dr. Barr insisted that we get some psychiatric training, and the only way that could be done was for us to make rounds with a psychiatrist from India who insisted on conducting the teaching sessions at noon on Fridays, once a month, which coincided with our only lunchtime. So we nicknamed the psychiatrist the Noon Balloon from Rangoon. (Yes, he was considerably overweight.)

Another incident of interest was that a sixty-year-old guy named David Florence, in Boston, died, and I am pleased to report that I received many condolences in the mail. To keep life interesting, we had an exchange resident physician from Spain whose first name was Fernando. Dr. Barr did not like the way Fernando closed wounds, so he asked me to show Fernando our way of doing the task. Well, Fernando was highly insulted and his honor was at stake, so he challenged Dr. Barr to a duel. I did some fancy international phoning and Fernando was gone in a week. Dr. Barr thought it was funny but I did not, having grown up in the underworld.

There were additional moments of humor, such as when the North East Airlines crash occurred on Nantucket Island. Yes, there was a North East Airlines in those days, and this was one of the situations that eventually led to its demise. The survivors were all flown to Massachusetts General Hospital, where we opened up a special unit in the Baker building to care for them. I stayed there 24/7 and ran the show. A Jewish mother of a young woman in her twenties decided that I should be the girl's husband. Despite showing her pictures of my wife and three children, it was to no avail as she had her mind made up. Thank God, the rabbi came to my rescue.

My moment of international fame came when a very prominent internist from London was sent to Dr. Barr because of unrelenting low back pain that was determined not to be a disc. In those days we did do myelograms and his was normal, so Dr. Barr turned him over to me. I listened earnestly to the patient's long and agonizing story. One point hit my brain like a ton of bricks, and that was that this doctor's low back pain was much worse at night and he couldn't get a good night's rest even with pills, which is what precipitated the transoceanic flight for relief. I therefore speculated osteoid osteoma (a benign bone tumor) and ordered serial oblique cuts on x-rays of the low back, and there it was on the pedicle, and a very large one at that. It had the typical ring around the nidus, although I realized that the patient was older than the age group usually encountered for this tumor. I made the diagnosis and ultimately did the surgery, resulting in complete relief of the patient's pain, and thus obtained three days of international fame (you have to take it when you can get it).

In 1961 the draft board paid me a visit, and I'm sure it was because of my very unique "good looks" that I became a member of the U.S. Army. We had very serious grand rounds every week at Massachusetts General Hospital, and a fellow resident, Scoot Dimon, and I introduced humor into that very stale and sophisticated atmosphere. On the last day of my presentation at the grand rounds, Dr. Eugene Record (part of the orthopedic group) praised Scoot and I for the transition, and also pointed out that we had doubled the attendance at the famous Massachusetts General grand orthopedic rounds in just one year's time.

I can truly state that I enjoyed every minute of my time at Massachusetts General Hospital and had every intention of returning to the practice group.

However, Dr. Barr died in 1962 and the group broke up. My next return to Boston was in October 2016, when Dr. Joseph Barr, Jr. and I exchanged memories. We still keep in frequent touch by email. You might say that he is my adopted brother since I consider his father as my adopted father. Thus the tradition continues.

Chapter 9

After eleven months in Dr. Barr's private practice group, the call of the U.S. Army occurred. I had been able to delay the process through the Berry Plan, whereby doctors who were taking their residency were deferred from registering with Selective Service, but I ran out of time. Having three children was not an impediment, and orthopedic surgeons were in demand because of the Vietnam War.

My desire was to be assigned to West Point, where there was an opening, but one of my fellow residents at the Harvard program for one year had been an army veteran of sixteen years, so he took that choice assignment. I was chosen to go to Fort Benning, Georgia for basic training. However, the presiding orthopod at Fort Huachuca in Arizona was sent to Vietnam, so I had an "emergency assignment" to go to Fort Huachuca to take his place, resulting in my bypass of basic training.

I arrived at Fort Huachuca in southern Arizona with my wife and three children, being assigned to 110 Jeffords Street in the noncommissioned officers' area. I had no problem being in the NCO area, but after a month I was told that I was to move to the newer officers' section called Wherry. By that time we were well settled in and liked our neighbors, so I put up a big fight that went all the way up to the general's office, where the general's wife made the decision that I could stay at 110 Jeffords. Obviously she had a personality like mine, and we were friends for life (as will come out subsequently).

So there I was at Fort Huachuca with no basic training, no uniforms and no formal army training. In essence I was not certain of what format to follow, so I merely followed my instincts. So what was this Fort Huachuca place surrounded by giant satellite dishes and a highly restricted area? It so happens that Fort Huachuca was the U.S. Army's Electronic Warfare and Intelligence Centers and was the largest U.S. military reservation in the nation, extending from Sierra Vista, Arizona to Yuma, Arizona, thereby facilitating the development of early pilotless drones and heat-seeking missiles, along with adequate space to test them. Fort Huachuca was originally established to control the Apache Indian Nation because of the multiple uprisings of the various tribes. Names like Geronimo and Cochise were at the top of the list. The tribes in the immediate Fort Huachuca region were known as Chiricahua, ultimately displaced to Oklahoma and Florida.

So how did this move affect my family? My fourth child, Sharon, was born in Fort Huachuca, and her siblings repeatedly informed her that she was an Indian because of this fact. The misperception stuck and Sharon was a teenager before she realized the fallacy.

Speaking of Sharon and as a note of humor, she had three older siblings all under age five (a real crew). At the time of her baptism in the Catholic Church as an infant, the entire family proceeded to a small wooden Catholic chapel and sat neatly in our seats when the priest entered, the lighted candle being held by an altar boy. We all subsequently stood up and the children spontaneously blurted out "happy birthday" in song. Even the priest broke up.

So just what was my job at Fort Huachuca? I discovered I was the only orthopedic surgeon for the Army and the Air Force between El Paso, Texas and San Diego, California, which bases had their respective major military hospital facilities. Therefore my responsibilities included both Luke and Davis-Monthan Air Force Bases, but I was specifically assigned to Fort Huachuca. I also found out that my general surgical training and experience was greatly needed, since the assigned general surgeon at Fort Huachuca did have some medical problems.

I rarely left the base except for a few temporary duty assignments (TDYs), and one afternoon a month I was permitted to go to the crippled children's clinic in Tucson ninety miles away, as I was on call 24/7 for two and a half years and simply did not have the liberty to leave. Also, I did not take any vacation time since there was no replacement. Therefore, besides orthopedic duties I also did general surgical cases as above described, plus took MOD (medical officer of the day) call once a week at night plus every fourth weekend. I was capable of covering all specialties except OB/GYN and pediatrics, so my rotating internship paid off.

Fort Huachuca proved to be a very interesting series of events. I was no war hero but I'll let you decide the adventure level. Certain individuals played key roles in my survival, and one of the first and foremost was my neighbor, the sergeant major. Now, for those of you without military experience, I will explain that the sergeant major is the highest ranking NCO on the base and is addressed as "Major" even though he is not a commissioned officer. The major was a handsome black man with a sparkling personality, and we got along super great. He and I would discuss problems by the hour in an effort to solve the difficulties which were at times overwhelming. We were dealing with a drafted population, and without question some were definitely behavioral disorders. The inductees were from all over the nation. Some came from very rural areas and had not been vaccinated against infectious diseases, which resulted in periodic waves of measles, mumps, chickenpox, and just about everything else. I had one ward for contagious diseases but the patients were not isolated, so that meant that the kids with measles were exposed to those with other infectious diseases. Sometimes the spreading was nonstop. Therefore, whatever contagious disease was on special that week could be expected to spread through the ward, hitting those who did not have any type of resistance or immunity. I can remember one time frame when three guys in a row had mumps, and the size of their testicles would challenge cantaloupes. They all prayed to die.

However, the sickest boy that I can remember had herpes zoster, which is the same virus as chickenpox. He could not even tolerate the sheets to touch his skin, so we built a tent over his bed and used heavy sedation for four days until he could eat by mouth.

I had three corpsmen assigned to me, but became especially attached to one named Hoogens. He was from the coal mining area in West Virginia and had a great accent, plus his skill level amazed me. You only had to show or tell him something once and it stuck.

Hoogens was best remembered by the following saga. To do my job well I had to be highly organized and very efficient, and that I was. As stated before, I did have to share night and weekend call, following which I was required to meet with the commanding officer of the hospital the following morning. One morning after MOD, Hoogens and I appeared before Col. La Bossi and I properly saluted. Col. LaBossi addressed Hoogens directly, asking, "Hoogens, does Capt. Florence have things organized?"

In his magnificent West Virginia twang Hoogens replied, "Sir, if you knows the Capt., even his bowel movements is organized."

I had never seen Col. LaBossi laugh before, but he broke up and responded, "Enough said." It is true that I ran my section with an iron hand, but I was always respectful to all my staff and patients.

As an additional point of interest, I did feel that the food at the hospital unit was better than the general mess on the main base. I actually enjoyed the food and would congratulate the mess sergeants and the cooks after each meal. My reward was a very nicely packed lunch for every night that I was on call. The other doctors could not figure out why I got special treatment.

As a point of humor, at the time of the Vietnam War there was a Mexican song (we were actually only a short distance from the border) that could be heard coming from Mexican radio stations called the "Mexican Hat Dance," during which clapping of the hands was part of the format. Well, my children renamed the song the "Mexican clap dance." That misnomer was more accurate than generally perceived, since Fort Huachuca had the highest venereal disease rate of any military installation in the United States, and the slang name for the most prevalent disease was "the clap."

One of the jobs that the sergeant major and I had to do was visit the town of Aqua Prieta, across the border in Mexico, and bring back the bodies of the dead recruits who either died of drinking rotgut alcohol in the bars or from cardiac failure in the whorehouses. A total of six were retrieved during my time, plus seven who died at an abrupt turn in the road on the way back, not realizing that the road did not accommodate a car going eighty mph. Many of the draftees had very little common sense and little immunity to disease.

There were also some elements of total stupidity. As described in my previous book, the sheriff of Cochise County (who lived in back of me on the base) told me that one of his deputies had stopped a pickup truck, heading to the base from Mexico, loaded with cases of "good whiskey." I chose to keep my mouth shut, as I came from a culture where you don't "sing or squeal." While the boys got away with the trick for a while, they became more risky and got caught by the MPs for selling the stuff in the NCO club without having paid a federal tax. To my surprise, all seven were convicted and sent to Leavenworth Federal Prison in Kansas, where I subsequently visited them later in my military career.

Chapter 10

The epitome of disasters occurred during my second year at Fort Huachuca. I developed a friendship with a young first lieutenant who worked in a highly classified service office. He called me one night, requesting an immediate meeting at his office. He let me in by the code and showed me an unlocked drawer that should have been locked and which he had checked before he left the previous day. He was a career officer and felt that his goose was cooked, as the blame would fall on him. He called the MIC (Military Intelligence Center) and I stayed with him when the entourage arrived. The problem was greater than I had initially perceived. MIC did not feel that the lieutenant was the culprit, and both he and I were allowed to go home with a "mouth shut command."

This event occurred on a Sunday night and I stewed most of the night with only intermittent sleep. Tuesday morning I was working in the emergency department when Hoogens ran in from the inpatient building and said that I had a call from the general's office, ordering me to be at the ER entrance ASAP. I didn't usually get calls from the general's office, so I knew that something big was up. I dropped what I was doing and headed for the ambulance entrance as two MP vehicles came flying around the corner with all lights flashing. The door of the first vehicle flew open and I jumped in as we proceeded to Colonels Row with lights and siren on.

The vehicle stopped at the home of the highest ranking individual on the base, who happened to be a male civilian, namely the person in charge of the highly secretive research project. I was hustled into the house and up the stairs

51

into the bedroom, where that guy (name suppressed) had obviously blown his head off. It was apparent that the pistol was placed in his mouth and fired, resulting in the entire back of his head being deposited on the bed.

Needless to say there was nothing I could do but assist in the placement of the body on the gurney (military stretcher) and head to the morgue. The news of the death on Colonels Row spread over the base, but I was told to keep my mouth shut and I did. Over the course of the next two months I was repeatedly interviewed by CIA and FBI agents, and they all asked the same questions. One CIA agent was particularly aggressive, so I concluded that the suicide was a big deal, and I was right.

Although general information was disseminated throughout the base, specifics were not. I eventually learned that the situation was espionage. However, I agreed with the agents to keep mute on the details, and even with my present senility I shall honor that military code today. I had again had a real taste of reality.

On a lighter note, I did temporarily solve a major problem, namely my youngest daughter was a climber and would not stay in her crib. So I borrowed the cargo netting from the back of a C-47 aircraft and placed it over the top of the crib. Her revenge was hanging on the netting with her fingers and screaming at the top of her voice. After receiving complaints from the neighbors, the netting was returned and 110 Jeffords was back to peace and quiet again.

I would say that the following is the closest I came, during my time at Fort Huachuca, to doing something heroic. I loved to fly and needed something to do as a diversion. Well, the original helicopter at Fort Huachuca was the Bell Iroquois, which was used to lay cable from low altitude. The Iroquois led to the Huey which was starting in service in Vietnam. The two-blade prop of the Huey sounded like an eggbeater but it could do the job. I learned to fly copilot but could not do takeoffs or landings.

One Saturday afternoon I broke out of the clinic and went up in the Huey with my favorite pilot. We were well over the desert when I pointed out the sign on the dash which read, "Do not exceed 128 air miles per hour." So I asked, "What happens when you go faster than 128 air mph?" to which the pilot admitted that he did not know. Therefore we inched our way up the chain, smiling approvingly with each increment on the dash of the mph. At 142 air miles per hour the single sheet Plexiglas windshield dislodged and came into the cockpit, landing on the controls. This made it impossible to proceed forward. The pilot skillfully bellyflopped the thing with a sizable thud and we both got out, awaiting what we knew would be coming. As expected, it really hit the fan and the excuses we rendered didn't seem to help the situation at all. However, the flight engineer at the base got the brainstorm of putting a metal bar down the center of the windshield as a reinforcement and, praise the Lord, the airspeed was increased to 145 air miles per hour and we were exonerated (a little bit).

What other brilliant ideas did I have at Fort Huachuca? Well, I was on the way back from the crippled children's clinic in Tucson, and while driving through the mountains I saw an animal corpse in the road being tended to by several vultures. I had never seen a vulture up close, so I stopped the car, got out, and walked over to the corpse, and the birds took off and circled overhead. What I didn't know was that vultures would vomit on an intruder, and I was not the exception. I also found out that the puke smell was permanent and could not be removed from clothing by God or man. My nice dress uniform was discarded.

Since my trips to Tucson were my only bail from the base, I was again returning from the crippled children's clinic after a heavy cloudburst had occurred in the mountains, and as I was driving on the narrow plateau I heard a tremendous roar. I rolled down the window but wisely stayed in the old army Chevy. The sky was clear and as I looked up the narrow canyon, I saw a wall of water coming down. I quickly moved the car, got out and watched the wall of water go by. Yes, I had seen my first arroyo.

I spent many hours in the hospital clinic, but one of my most unforgettable patients was a woman who had been in a Nazi ghetto concentration camp during World War II, and the distal one-third of all her fingers and thumbs were black exposed bone. I offered to do the needed surgery, but she informed me that her mission was to show humanity how much she had suffered. I must say, she was effective.

Fort Huachuca had some basic recruits, but not large numbers. An important part of the indoctrination was an education on the endemic insects and reptiles, most of them harmless unless you taunt them, so one learned not to agitate the rattlers or particularly the colorful coral snakes. One of the caveats to the novices was not to defecate on a log in the forest, as baby rattlers live under those logs and are butt biters. One kid from the Bronx laughed at the whole thing, and guess who came into the clinic a few days later with several small and painful bite marks on the butt?

One of the very few off-base missions that I served occurred one weekday afternoon when I was again in the clinic and received a call from the general's office requesting my immediate departure to Luke Air Force Base. In brief, a fighter plane pilot and trainee had crashed. Both survived but had significant leg fractures, and the physicians at the base wanted an orthopedist to stabilize both patients before they were able to be airvac'd to Naval Medical Center San Diego. We were there in no time via the general's plane. I did my thing then, and because of my love of aviation, had a tour of the base. Several of the trainees were from foreign countries, and I was very surprised to learn that the highest percentage of training crashes was by German pilots. I would have determined otherwise.

My stories of Fort Huachuca could go on forever, but let's move on. At the end of my two years of duty I had taken no vacation, so I moved my family to Minneapolis on what was called terminal leave and still on army time. Wouldn't you know, I came down with infectious mononucleosis, and was thus reactivated and sent to Fort Leavenworth to recover, work in the clinic, and serve additional time. The entire process took another three months, during which time relatives had to help out with family while I toiled in the outpatient clinic. I did manage to shoot up to the federal penitentiary in Leavenworth, Kansas to see my old MP friends who had been selling the illegal whiskey, and I accomplished this by volunteering to staff the orthopedic clinic at the penitentiary for one week. When finally discharged I proceeded back to Minneapolis, but the mononucleosis took several more weeks to totally dissipate.

Chapter 11

So why did I choose Minneapolis when I had never lived there before and knew no one except one pastor and his family? Well, I was tired of the desert and the heat, and I wanted to go as far north as I could in America and still be in the U.S., plus have the potential for practice in a sizable community. I chose a small clinic in St. Louis Park, Minnesota, a suburb of Minneapolis, and lived in a rural rental facility where the plumbing was a big problem from day one. North Memorial Hospital had just opened its sizable new facility, and I was working between Methodist and North Memorial Hospitals as an orthopedic traumatologist.

On one of my trips between the two hospitals I encountered a major one-car accident, where the vehicle had hit a steel railroad abutment near Highways 55 and 100. The occupant was unconscious and blue, but both the driver and passenger doors were locked. I had a stiletto and a small hammer in my trunk, so I mosaiced the passenger window and pushed it in, unlocked the door and jumped into the vehicle, putting the occupant's head back and pounding on his chest. Miraculously he woke up and started breathing, and at that point a parade of emergency vehicles arrived and took over. Ironically, the patient was a postal worker from the Golden Valley post office who eventually ended up being my mailman after I built a home in Golden Valley.

North Memorial Hospital got busier and busier, and I was running back and forth twelve to fourteen hours a day when the administrator of North Memorial, Vance DeMong, convinced me to move to Robbinsdale, Minnesota, where I rented a home about two blocks from the hospital. Instead of decreasing my work hours, the same significantly increased, since the emergency department staff knew that I was available.

North Memorial rapidly became a trauma center along with the Hennepin County Medical Center and St. Paul Ramsey. I opened an office across from North Memorial Hospital and was looking for help within four months. My group eventually expanded to five orthopedic physicians, but I continued to stay in touch with my underworld contacts who were long-term friends. One of the classic scenarios is described in my former book relative to the mafia boss from Chicago. He sent his wife to me relative to the issue of a disc in her lower back for which I eventually did surgery, and I also carefully realigned the beautiful multicolor tattoo on her back so that the scar would not be apparent. However, as the story unfolds, the mob boss denied knowledge of the tattoo, leaving myself feeling like a penny waiting for change. I must admit it was a beautiful tattoo.

About one year after opening the practice, my business manager informed me that the St. Croix Falls clinic needed orthopedic consultation services, so I began monthly treks to St. Croix Falls, Wisconsin, and it was on one of those trips that I was asked to see Elvis Presley at Hazleton. The scenario is described subsequently in this book, and I genuinely mourned his subsequent death in 1977 at the young age of forty-two, as he was truly a talented artist.

Interestingly enough, as a child I was always very interested in the Ohio State Police, since I grew up in Ohio. I was fascinated with that rotating red light on the top of their vehicle and used every opportunity to communicate with the officers in various settings. After getting out of the army during the Vietnam era and opening a practice in Minnesota, through a friend I got to know Sgt. Tom Turney, the officer in charge of training for the Minnesota Highway Patrol. Training films were needed and I had just gotten my feet wet in the film industry doing a production with Sheri Lewis and her puppet Hush Puppy in a film titled *Hush Puppy's Bright Idea*, a safety film for instruction of children. Subsequently, all of my free time was spent making training films for police and fire use, such as EOB (how to deliver a baby), which is ironic since I had spent so much effort avoiding that specialty during my formal training. A very popular film was *Extrication Rescue*, which instructed fire and police personnel on how to use the newly discovered "jaws of life." I also participated in a course titled "Police Pursuit-Safely," and to do this I had to fulfill the following training courses at the St. Cloud State Police training facility in July

1974: "Advanced Driving Technique-Pursuit," and "Collision Avoidance in Pursuit." Since I had previously tested racecars for Firestone Tire and Rubber Company in Akron, the speed did not perturb me, and ironically I did better than the officers on the first day, but then they surpassed my skill level on subsequent days when they were more at ease. The Safety Sidearms course was also accomplished, and I did receive a certificate for completion of these courses. However, the plaque of which I am most proud is a colorful Minnesota Rescue and First Aid Association, 1970, which is proudly displayed in my living room titled, "Physician of the Year-Minnesota."

Sergeant Turney retired and opened the Turncraft Clock Shop in Golden Valley, Minnesota, and we continued to be close friends. He was truly one of the finest associates of my lifetime. As my adventures progressed, I continued my involvement with the highway patrol in the states of Ohio, Michigan and Pennsylvania.

Speaking of rescue and the "jaws of life," my parents were in a senior citizens' facility in Canton, Ohio in the mid-1960s, and trips with the family were very few because of my busy schedule. We were staying in the Lawson Motel, which my father had designed as an architect. This was the first and last venture of the Lawson Dairy Company into the motel business. On a beautiful summer day at the motel, my children were in the pool and I was just putting on my swim trunks when my oldest daughter Julie came running into the room to tell me that there had been a big car crash outside the motel. In my slippers and swim trunks I ran to the front door, and her statement was not an exaggeration. One car was on its side in the road but that driver was able to get out. The second car was in the field across the street, where it was upright and two men were trying, and failing, to get the locked doors opened.

As I approached the two-door sedan, I could see that the single occupant appeared to be a young male slumped over the steering wheel and definitely blue in color. It was obvious that he was not breathing. The two men backed away as I took a rock and tried to break the windshield, but was unsuccessful as it only cracked. I had less success on the side windows so I turned my attention to the rear window, which I pulverized with several large blows of rocks. With the jagged glass as the residual, I laboriously climbed in through the shattered rear window, cutting myself with several smaller lacerations on the arms and a larger gash of the right thigh. I got to the boy, pulled his head back and immediately started mouth-to-mouth breathing. Miraculously in about thirty seconds he groaned and gasped, followed by a deep breath and breathing on his own.

By this time three Canton police cars and a fire truck arrived, pried open the driver's door and extracted both the boy and myself. Within a few minutes a Canton fire ambulance arrived and oxygen was immediately applied as the ambulance transported the boy and myself to Altman Hospital. Considerable and understandable attention was focused on the boy, whereas I was put in a side room to be stitched up by a fellow who had been a corpsman in the army. Therefore we talked army shop while he sewed me up. After my minor procedures I was driven by a police vehicle back to the motel and, needless to say, I could not go into the pool. I did not realize at the time that no information about myself had been taken at the hospital relative to identification.

My always eventful life continued over the next three years at its usual hundred miles-per-hour pace, and on one Saturday morning at my home on 205 South Rhode Island in Golden Valley, Minnesota there was a knock on the door. A middle-aged man and woman asked to see Dr. Florence. When I acknowledged that I was that individual, I hardly got the word out of my mouth when the woman grabbed me and held me tight, weeping profusely. They were the boy's parents and they had searched for me for three years, finally hiring a private detective to do the job. I must say this was a wonderful reunion, as I also was very thrilled with their presence.

Right about the same time a significant disaster occurred. To give the background of the problem (and I will not use his name), a young general surgeon had started at North Memorial Hospital at about the same time I did. Myself being an orthopedic traumatologist, and he being a general surgeon in a new practice, we both had several encounters in treating mutual patients. We both had a sizable young family, and our families became friends. Things seemed to work relatively well until definite behavioral changes were noted after about one year of practice. I also was informed that he had had some surgical complications, but the epitome apparently occurred when he had a major complication with a relative of one of the Twin Cities area mafia bosses.

It was about 11:30 at night and I was already in bed when the phone rang, the person on the other end of the line demanding I come to the Lexington Hotel in Minneapolis as soon as possible. The call was definitely from the "friends" and truly was an unusual contact. I had to have some excuse to tell my wife, so I informed her that the training doctors at the hospital were having a party and were wondering why I was not there. The excuse was anemic, but I quickly dressed and proceeded to the hotel, where I was informed that the surgical complication had resulted in death, and my own opinion relative to the next step was requested. The level of unhappiness was quite apparent and I was told that retribution was necessary. At that point I asked to take over the situation, knowing that the doctor involved had had a drug problem, but I was only given thirty days to solve the present issue. I therefore met with the offender, who admitted to the use of drugs in his life, along with other problems. Not wishing to request the demise of a friend, I reached an agreement with the surgeon to leave the state. He agreed to do so and moved to an adjacent state, where he got involved with a girlfriend and a motorcycle group. I did not know his immediate destination but did find out several months later that he was killed in an accident while riding his motorcycle. The task, therefore, was completed without my intervention. I again invoked the 11th Commandment, "Do not feel bad when bad things happen to bad people."

As a change of tone, I will relate that I took my six children to a ranch in Wyoming where they could ride horseback and herd cattle. In actuality, on such ranches you simply ride the horses, and dogs control the cattle with minimal cowboy input. I was very proud of my youngest six-year-old daughter Renée, who was on her horse every morning while other alternating children chose to remain in bed.

One night the sheriff came to the camp to inform me that there had been a major accident when a pickup truck with three people came over a hill and hit a herd of cattle. I was asked to help sort the human from the animal carnage, and I must admit it was a chore. I thought we had done a good job, but I was subsequently informed by one of the ranch hands who attended the funeral of the victims that he had heard a "mooing" sound coming out of one of the caskets. Obviously our job of sorting was not definitive.

Chapter 12

It was in 1967, on a Saturday morning after orthopedic grand rounds at the University of Minnesota, when Dr. John Moe, the chief professor of orthopedic surgery at the university, took me aside to make an unusual request. To give you some background, Dr. Moe was not only the chief, but in my eyes he was my adopted father, similar to Dr. Barr, showing considerably more interest in me than I had experienced previously in life from my own father.

The request was unique in that he was asking me to make a venture that had not been satisfactorily accomplished previously. There was a worldwide refugee food service called CARE and an offshoot medical entity called Medico (actually the residual of the Vietnam medical service established by the famous Tom Dooley—remember the song?). The two entities had merged and previous attempts to meet the needs in Afghanistan had not materialized due to the apprehension of the two prior orthopedic surgeons assigned to Afghanistan, primarily relative to the problems and complications of TB orthopedic spine and joint disease. Tuberculosis was quite prevalent in the nation of Afghanistan, and efforts to control it had not been even reasonably successful.

Dr. Moe was aware of my fearless and brainless personality; however, realizing the risk to myself and family he had considerable doubt that I would consider going to Kabul. Needless to say I did go to Kabul, and thus entered a world that I could only imagine before. To go from a comfortable and organized existence to a land where the most critical needs were clean water, soap, and toilet paper was indeed a change. As I look back on the entire situation, I do not know how I did it except to fully acknowledge that a higher

61

power was with me. Although I will be going into greater detail of Afghanistan in a subsequent book, step inside and we will take a ride into a seemingly fantasy world that proved to me to be reality.

The trip was arranged and partially funded by the Shah of Iran, who was a good friend of Dr. Moe. My first stop was in Tehran, the capitol of Iran, during the two thousand five hundredth anniversary of that city. Yes, I said twenty-five hundred, and the Shah had ordered that every corner of the city be illuminated at nighttime. My only duties in Tehran would be to give a few lectures at the university, and I was therefore allowed to see select sights, including the world-famous Crown Jewels of Iran.

I might inject a note of humor by reporting that television had just come out to the public in Tehran, and it was not unusual to see men sitting on stools watching a small black and white TV showing American Western films. Owning a television was considered to be the epitome of accomplishment.

However, the next step was via Iran Air as I progressed to Kabul, Afghanistan. I can remember looking out of the window of the plane as we were landing and wondering if we were on the same planet. My speculations were correct in that the terrain appeared to be extra terrestial. Perception during a time of crisis is usually greater than the ultimate materialization, but Afghanistan was the exception. I lived in the U.S. government staff house, so at least I did get food. The quarters were adequate, but nothing was truly clean. I learned that I could not even brush my teeth with the water out of the faucet, as the drinking water came out of the adjacent river which was also the sewer.

The only meat was lamb prepared in various concoctions, and instead of orange juice we drank pomegranate juice until my eyeballs turned purple. Kabul was situated one mile high in the mountains, so fresh fruit and vegetables had to come from lower areas like Jalalabad. Kabul was still an ancient city, and no U.S. troops were present. The Russians had put together an army that was met at the northern border by the Northern Alliance, a coalition of multiple tribes, and the Soviets found they had truly met their match.

My job was to do multiple TB surgeries. Since my predecessors were apprehensive of tuberculosis, I lined up a full surgical schedule and did a case five mornings per week except on Thursday and Friday, which was the Muslim weekend and therefore I had to adjust in accordance. My surgical accomplishments were unbelievable, as I was routinely doing high risk transabdominal and transthoracic procedures which I had learned as a general surgeon. However, it did not take me long to appreciate that a higher power than myself was the major part of the project. For example, the OR windows had broken screens and flies were all over the place, including walking around the inside of the wounds in which I was operating. I did have to adjust to that environment, but I had an excellent first assistant nurse, Fatima, and my interpreter was my anesthesiologist, Dr. Ali. In reality both of these individuals were, in my opinion, living saints. I can remember one patient vomiting ascariasis worms all over the OR table, and Dr. Ali just cleaned them up and on we continued without batting an eye. By the way, an ascariasis worm is similar in size to American earthworms. TB pus was everywhere, but we merely mopped it up and kept going.

Even though stealing is an art form in Afghanistan, the few who are caught are punished by cutting off their right hand, and a very few would have their heads removed. Needless to say, those individuals were not subsequently seen in the clinic. Thieves who had a right hand amputation were seen in the clinic. Although loss of a hand may not seem like a problem relative to survival in the United States, I wish to point out that the lack of toilet paper in Afghanistan requires one to wipe himself with the left hand and reserve the right hand for eating, which was done communally as a social event. Therefore if you have only one hand you are isolated from society, and these victims frequently would commit suicide.

The smarter thieves didn't get caught. For example, my housekeeper at the U.S. government staff house was very sly in that he would place phony pills at the bottom of the vial which simulated the real medication. It took me a while to catch on to that one. However, the epitome of thievery, which I did not discover until I had left the staff house to return to America, was that he had taken every other traveler's check out of my packet. Again, I was long gone before discovering that little trick.

There were occasional notes of levity, such as the mattress fluffer who came down the road every Thursday morning singing his song. To understand the process, one must appreciate that the mattresses were merely stuffed with cotton, and if you wished the fluffer to fluff up your mattress, you simply threw it out the window (along with a coin of course). The fluffer would take the content and fluff it up with an instrument that looked like a bass violin. I do think that fantasy was an integral part of the process.

All shopping was done at the bizarre, which was a shoulder-to-shoulder deal, and you must hold onto your wallet at the same time. You could buy anything, new or stolen. Nuts were a staple food and were weighted on a balance scale with the human hand at the center. Needless to say, accuracy was a fantasy and multiple tricks were also used, such as placing chewing gum on the bottom of the pan on the vendor's side of the product. My best experience was when I approached the cheese booth and requested a pound of the black cheese. The vendor shooed away the flies and the cheese color turned to gray. Needless to say, I did not buy any cheese.

However, don't feel that the Afghans are not sportsmen. The national sport is called Buzkashi and consists of men on horseback vying for what they deem is a football, which in reality is a dead goat with the head and tail cut off, in a violent fight to grab the remaining legs and get the torso over the goal line. The crowd, representing various towns and tribes, goes wild. The day I was there only one player was killed, and that was considered to be a conservative game.

The miracle of miracles was that the patients did so well (at least during the three-month period that I was there), but again I will state very clearly that a higher power than myself performed most of the surgery, merely working through me as a physical agent. I did surgery on both adults and children, and again, tuberculosis of the spine, hips, and knees was by far the most prevalent. I was amazed at the lack of complications and/or infection that occurred in the patients, and a major portion of this phenomenon must be attributed to a very high level of immunity in the general population.

Since I could go on for hours about the experiences in Afghanistan, I will reserve that for a subsequent book, but at least the reader is able to get a taste of the total environment and situation from the few above stated comments.

I have been repeatedly asked whether Christianity and Islam can reasonably blend. The answer is no. Christianity is based on love and Islam is based on obedience. I grew up in a Christian environment without love, but at the same time in an atmosphere of strict obedience, and thus I can relate to the Islamic approach as well. For both cultures to blend one must have a common dictionary, and that does not exist between Christianity and Islam. Good and evil mean two different things in each of the cultures.

The next question invariably is can both coexist? The answer is yes, if tolerance is involved. At the present time radical elements of Islam are not demonstrating tolerance, and that damages the potential for the remaining workable segment.

The two religions are basically as different as oil and water, which are not miscible for a common end product. Please note that both oil and water are necessary to operate a gasoline engine, but cannot be mixed if one expects the engine to function. Compatibility requires "give" by both parties, and at present Islam is not flexible in certain countries and environments. There is an element of flexibility in Christianity, but the changes of policies and procedures may take hundreds of years. At present both ideologies are basically different, and the possibility of significant compromise may not be available during the limited time frame during which this planet will remain viable. However, I will note that I had absolutely no problem in dealing with the 100 percent Muslim population with which I lived and worked.

Chapter 13

About two years after working in Afghanistan I got a frantic call from CARE-MEDICO that the orthopedic volunteer for the Dominican Republic had backed out. With some last-minute changes and the addition of a new partner, I agreed to go for one month.

Well, the Dominican Republic was a fiasco. I was stationed in Santo Domingo and it was nothing like the pictures you see on Google today. It was actually a waste of time since I couldn't get anything organized and accomplished except the orthopedic clinic, and most of the complex surgery that I was supposed to be doing just didn't get done due to schedule changes and the disappearance of patients. Now, Franco Duvalier (also known as "Papa Doc" because he was a physician by profession) was President of Haiti at that time (the other side of the island), and maybe he was kidnapping some of the patients. In any case, I will never know except to say that I was so frustrated that after three weeks I came home, having paid for the trip myself.

However, it wasn't all bad. I had a cook for three meals a day and she was good. My amusement came from watching the five chameleons that took care of the flies in my apartment, since the shuttered windows had no screens. Also, Santo Domingo got its first modern fire engine during my stay and the firemen spent three days driving the thing all over town with the red lights and siren on full tilt. Crowds lined the streets to help in the celebration.

I did take an afternoon off to go swimming in the ocean, but the stint was short when I surfaced to face a floating turd. That ended my swim. Also the electricity was allocated to various parts of town throughout the day, and since the water was on electrical dependence, showers had to be carefully planned.

The weekend activities began at noon on Friday and continued until noon on Monday to give everyone a chance to sober up from the huge rum consumption. I did learn a very important lesson relative to sugarcane in that the young boys on the island constantly chewed on sugarcane leaves and their teeth were sparkling white. Then off went the sugarcane to the La Romana refinery down the road, and after that process the natives rarely touched the sugar except to make rum. So in essence, non-refined sugar is not a toxin or health hazard.

So back to Minnesota I went, and being a member of the Minnesota National Guard we were assigned to a winter training session at Camp Ripley in northern Minnesota with a Norwegian contingent. I was amazed with the fact that the Norwegian men and women slept together, but I thought it was a great idea. Little did I know that in 1986 when I was with NATO troops in Germany, we also would fall under the same aegis in a gymnasium, wearing heavy fatigues twenty-four hours a day and barely able to move, much less exploit. Yet, the fun group to watch was a reserve unit from California also sent to Camp Ripley for winter training when it was forty to sixty degrees below zero. The only productivity the people in the group could manifest was to stand in one spot, quiver and shake and voraciously complain. A few of the members thought that death was imminent.

My life took a series of rapidly developing events in 1971 when I was asked to help develop the orthopedic trauma program at St. Paul-Ramsey Hospital in St. Paul Minnesota. I went from the frying pan into the fire for two years, pursuing a ridiculous schedule and a long commute. We started out with three orthopedists, but after one orthopedist was shot and killed by his wife, the remaining two of us had to do more than a yeoman's job. However I did not last, in that after two years I developed a full-blown fibromyalgia and reached the point of nonfunctioning.

I subsequently rested for a few months, and then went to school at the University of Minnesota to get degrees in law and public administration. While I flunked out of law school (for many reasons), I did get the public administration degree with the intention of pursuing healthcare administration as a career. I functioned in various lesser capacities until 1979, when I was asked to take the position of founder and director of the chronic pain rehabilitation program at the Sister Kenny Institute in Minneapolis. Thus I became one of the pioneers in the field of chronic pain diagnosis and treatment. The job had its ups and downs, but I had a good staff and we did accomplish a considerable amount during those pioneer years. The majority of the patients were of workers' compensation origin; some of them wanted to get rid of their pain and get better, and others did not. I soon learned that pain is a very ethereal entity.

One very unhappy patient was named Sam. He graduated from the program with a poor report card and an edict from his insurance company to return to work, but the command did not set well. One evening I was home and got a phone call from Sam, threatening my life. I thought a while and the next day spoke to the chief of police of Golden Valley, Minnesota, who told me the bad news that there was nothing I could do on merely a verbal threat. One week later, on a Saturday morning, Sam called again and this time talked to my youngest daughter, Renée, threatening to kill her and the whole family. He told her that she would, "fit perfectly inside a container." I took this threat very seriously and contacted my mafia connection in the Twin Cities. After an in-depth explanation of the problem, I was assured that "it will be taken care of." Three days later I got a phone call stating to me, "It's all done." The same day in the *Minneapolis Star Tribune* a brief article appeared about the bound body found in the Minnesota River accompanied by three bullet holes. I could finally relax, and at this point I invoked the 11th Commandment.

I continued in the pain rehabilitation business until 1986, when I was offered the position of chief of medical rehabilitation services, Industrial Commission of Ohio, which was totally a state controlled system. My appointment was by the governor and my boss was a physician named Ernie Johnson, M.D., associate dean of the College of Medicine at Ohio State University in the rehabilitation field. Dr. Johnson was wonderful to work with, and he also assigned me as a part-time medical legal consultant to the Social Security Court of Appeals in Columbus, but that was the end of the benefits. The facility to which I was assigned was the newly opened magnificent $18-million J. Leonard Camera Rehabilitation Center, and what more could a guy want? However, again I had a brutal lesson in political reality. I needed sixteen physical therapists and apparently over fifty were interviewed. I waited for the results, but after three months of nothing happening I confronted the very young director of the project. He informed me that the applicants' voting records were being reviewed. When I pointed out that such a process was totally illegal, he just smiled. That was just the beginning of an impossible situation.

I had actually joined the Ohio National Guard Regional Command Center to give the mess at the rehab facility a chance to settle down. I volunteered to go with a medical unit to a NATO assignment in Germany for several months. This was 1986, three years before the Berlin wall came down, and we were to be stationed at the Fulda Gap. The flight over was a nightmare, as this was before the military had put the brakes on smoking on military aircraft, and I had severe bronchitis both coming and going.

While in Germany we did essentially nothing and therefore I had to find my own tasks and procedures of interest, one of which was testing irradiated milk which did not require refrigeration. Therefore, I would fill up my fatigue pockets at every opportunity, giving a visual impression that I was loaded with ammunition.

As points of interest, we were told to avoid the large ant hills in the farm fields with our tanks, since the Germans used ants instead of insecticides. We moved the Abrams M1 tanks on the Autobahn at nighttime to minimize traffic interruptions, and rubber treads were used to minimize the road surface damage. All tanks had large flashing yellow lights on top which were activated with any mobility. I was not in that tank, but was told the following morning that a German Audi with four occupants had hit the back of a moving tank on the Autobahn. All four people in the car were killed. The tanker driver thought it was just a clunk in the engine and never stopped to explore, and was therefore told of the reality the following morning.

Most of the time we slept in our fatigues in a large gymnasium, both the men and the women, except for a few days when I stayed in an old German horse cavalry barn, my gear tied to one of the horse rope rings on the wall. A very educational three days was spent when I accompanied an American soldier from World War II who had married a German girl and stayed in Germany as a policeman, primarily in a cruiser on the Autobahn. The German police are quite rigid in their procedures. Those were the three most enjoyable days of the entire venture, and I admit that I actually learned something.

My Ohio National Guard medical unit had just returned to Columbus from our NATO assignment in Germany and we were scheduled for target training at the National Guard base. Officers were required to carry a 45-caliber pistol. However, I was never able to use a 45 since my hand was too small to control the apparatus. I was therefore permitted to carry a 38-caliber pistol with which I could both reasonably operate and hit a target. One Saturday morning my 38 was in for repairs, and I had borrowed a Beretta from a friend and had used it at target drill. During our tour in Germany we had only two sets of fatigue uniforms, and I had worn out one pair so I purchased a second at the drill that morning after target practice. I then stopped at a tailor shop earlier that afternoon, needing adjustments to the new fatigues. I was standing on a measurement pedestal in my underwear when a guy came flying through the door with a pistol, shouting in a Middle Eastern accent, "Deese ease stickup."

Now, who would hold up a tailor shop on a Saturday afternoon? Either a prank or a nut. The situation ultimately turned out to be the latter. The man told LeTous, the tailor, to give him money from the cash register and told me to get my wallet. I still wasn't sure what the hell was going on, so I got off the measuring pedestal and went into the change room, taking out my wallet and at the same time taking the small size Beretta pistol out of its holster. I draped the wallet over the pistol and proceeded back to the encounter. While the intruder pointed his pistol at my head with his right hand, I finally realized that this was real. I held out the wallet-covered Beretta with my right hand, and as he reached to grab the wallet I fired two quick shots, both of which hit him in the abdomen. He fell to his knees, looked up at me and then fell over sideways, hitting his head on the leg of a table. Subsequently he lay motionless. I thought I had hit a vital organ and that school was out.

LeTous stuck his head up over the counter and smiled. I did not smile in return but picked up the phone, punched zero and said to the operator, "This is Col. Florence and I've just shot a burglar."

The response from the operator was, "What?" After repeating the request for assistance, I just stood in place in my underwear. After about two minutes the air was filled with the sound of sirens, and two policemen came charging through the front door with guns drawn. I tried to explain the situation but there was simply too much confusion. After about three more minutes a fire engine and fire ambulance arrived, and the victim woke up and was carted away on a gurney. I got dressed and in about twenty minutes the chief of police arrived, and he was satisfied with my explanation. However, after another forty-five minutes the commanding general of the National Guard arrived and he was very unhappy.

After hearing the total story, I was repeatedly admonished with, "Colonel, you know the regulations."

I repeatedly responded with, "Yes, sir," because I knew I was wrong to take a loaded weapon off the drill field. However, it's important to note that neither the pistol nor the ammunition were classified as military issue.

I drove back to my townhouse with considerable concern in that I did not know a reasonable next step. The robber survived but did lose one kidney. I had gone back to work the following Monday, still in a state of quandary, and on Tuesday I got a phone call from the governor's office telling me, "Nothing happened; the incident did not occur." I somehow was not assured by that caveat.

After reciting the 11th Commandment repeatedly to myself, I knew that problems would develop, so I immediately called the headhunter who got me the job in Columbus, and I requested a different assignment. Actually, an aide in the governor's office worked with that headhunter to help me get my next government job, which was in the greater Detroit area.

Chapter 14

Talk about jumping from the frying pan into the fire, I took the job of Medical Director for the People's Community Hospital Authority of Michigan (greater Detroit area) consisting of Wayne, Annapolis, Outer Drive, Seaway and Oakwood Hospitals. PCHA had been set up during the Second World War to meet the needs of the massive migration to the Detroit area of workers for the war plants. The hospitals were owned and operated by the State of Michigan and administrated by a board of about fourteen members, actually politicians and union bosses. I am pleased to state that this board was the most reasonable and attentive that I have ever worked for and with.

One gigantic problem was that since the hospitals were state owned and controlled, any licensed physician in Michigan with a valid medical license was eligible for staff privileges. So guess where some of the bad guys went? One physician on Friday afternoons would stand in the driveway of his office and write narcotic prescriptions for a fee (doesn't that sound like today). Well, the feds got him. Another physician, who was a very smooth surgeon, had been involved in a suspicious situation with the death of his girlfriend, who was also a patient. The problems with the various physicians were such that the sheriff's office used me as an undercover agent. I can tell you that was quite an experience, which I have agreed not to discuss.

The Detroit area was very different but I worked very hard. I did a good job (as I was later told), but needed to get out of government employment. So after three years in Detroit (from 1986 to 1989), I took the job of vice president of medical affairs of a medical complex named Polyclinic in Harrisburg,

Pennsylvania. The private sector was refreshing but boring. One of my community service jobs was that of president of the Board of Health of the City of Harrisburg, and this enabled me to park in the mayor's spot for my evening meetings. Illicit drugs were becoming popular, and to avoid boredom I functioned as an undercover agent for the Commonwealth of Pennsylvania, Bureau of Professional Affairs. I became notorious after cracking a case ultimately titled, "The Special Chicken" (otherwise known as "The Cocaine Chicken Special"), where a fast food joint offered the "hot stuff" under an order of chicken in a paper cup with a napkin covering the cocaine. All I had to do was ask for the "special chicken" and guess what I got?

After eight years in Harrisburg developing many wonderful relationships with physicians and associates, I decided to semi-retire and in 1997 moved to a small country estate outside of Eau Claire, Wisconsin. After about a year I got bored and joined an expanding medical group in Eau Claire named the Marshfield Clinic, where I remained from 1998 to 2004. Following 2004, I moved back to the Twin Cities of Minnesota for further adventures. Two of my former students needed assistance in their clinic, so I helped them out for a year before rejoining a previous associate in private practice in St. Paul. There was little opportunity for levity in my existence, so I used the communal relationship that arose in the elevator between my office and a medical clinic that catered primarily to an older population. For a change of pace I relate a couple of those stories.

One afternoon I joined two elderly ladies in the elevator and politely asked them, "what floor," to which their response was, "I don't know."

I quickly followed up with, "What color is the wall?" And the response was "green." So I pushed the second floor button and the door opened to green walls. As they walked out of the elevator I stated, "Take any car," and the response from the lady was, "Oh, thank you, sir."

I could go on forever, but here is my favorite: An elderly lady limped onto the elevator, and in a friendship venture I asked, "Bad hip?"

She responded, "It's my knees; they are shot and need replacement."

To demonstrate camaraderie I replied, "Yes, I have had three total knees."

She looked at me very quizzically and retorted, "But you only have two legs, where is the third one?" I was silent for a moment and then hastened to depart out of the next opening of the elevator door.

It was right about that time that I picked up a third wife. She had been a widow for five years and had a multicolor background. She hesitated to inform me that at one time she had sold appliances and that, in a state of confusion, sold a five-year warranty for a compressor to a man purchasing a dishwasher. She was under stress at the time and still had guilty feelings about the issue after we got married, so I'm not the only crook in the family. She designed and supervised the construction of a lovely home in Hudson, Wisconsin in an area of early development, and we moved in during the summer of 2005.

One day I was at work in downtown St. Paul and she was gone from the house for two hours working as a volunteer in the local hospital. Upon returning to the house, it was obvious that the back of the home had been broken into and multiple items were stolen. A lack of neighbors at the time made the access easy and the security system had been scheduled for installation only three weeks later.

Being a vindictive individual, I vigorously pursued Hudson Police Department's case number A06.4636, along with the appropriate law enforcement individuals, and found out the name of the lady thief who tried to pawn some of our stuff in the Twin Cities. So I had a name. The robbery had occurred on 9-22-06, and the woman was discovered subsequently in an arrest in Peoria, Illinois for different issues. She was also found to be in possession of some of our stolen belongings. So I had my gal, but for multiple reasons could not get her extradited back to Hudson, Wisconsin, so I thought I was stuck. After much consternation and contemplation, I called my underworld connections in Chicago and placed a request for rehabilitation of the offending individual in Peoria, Illinois. The degree of rehabilitation was requested by my friends, and I responded with, "Total rehabilitation is needed." Ten days later I received a phone call stating that the rehabilitation had been completed. I asked no questions but merely stated, "thank you," and again recited the 11th Commandment.

I am now eighty-seven years old and have continued functioning as a medical legal consultant to industry, insurance companies, and attorneys in a declining business secondary to multiple mergers. With physical deterioration along with mental acceleration, I somehow keep going. Frequently I am asked whether a life like mine has led to "happiness." As an answer, I give you the following scenario to read, which I wrote two years ago, and you can make your own decision.

Happiness—Where Are You

I hear the word, and I see the shadow, but where are you.
Are you the mist that fades with the joy of life with it.
Are you the dark sky which shows a lone star that I cannot touch.
Are you the sound of the wind which touches me but quickly leaves.
Are you the joy I see in a child's face which quickly passes by.
Are you the sound of a bird's song that fades into the horizon.
Are you the petals of the flower which fade so quickly.
I reach for you but my fingertips elude your touch.
Why is it that I cannot find you—are you real.
Are you something that I merely hope for but cannot find.
Do you see me but turn away—am I real to you.
I walk slowly toward you but you run away.
I close my eyes and you are but a passing fantasy.
Should I really expect such a thing in this life or is it a dream.
I fabricate you in my mind but the pieces disappear.
I smell your fragrance but it quickly fades.
I walk your path but the pavement below me crumbles.
Is what I see in others something not destined for my existence.
Perhaps I can create you as an illusion and capture your fringes.
Are you real—or are you a perception or illusion.
Shall I try to create you in my fantasy and keep you as my own—
Or maybe it was just not intended to be.

Dr. David Trucker

People I Have Known

The Lone Ranger

It was 1965 and I was planning to build a home for my family in Golden Valley, Minnesota when on a Saturday afternoon I received a phone call from the builder Tom DeCola, requesting I come to his home to meet the person building the home next to my proposed home. I told Tom I would swing by on my way home from the hospital. I entered Tom's living room and saw a very handsome, tall man and when he opened his mouth, I heard the William Tell Overture in the back of my brain. One couldn't miss the unique and specific voice of the Lone Ranger.

His real name (theater name) was Clayton Moore, and after both homes were built, we became good friends. He moved to the Minneapolis area to be near his mother, who was in a nursing home in an adjacent community. He was in his sixties at the time; the years of movie and TV shows were all over, and he was making a living by doing personal appearances and rope tricks at various shows. Clayton was an accomplished showman, having been a circus acrobat at age eight and progressing to aerial trapeze acts plus other unique performances, even being a model for the prominent New York City based modeling agency Powers on occasion.

Since Clayton had done all of his own stunts in the films and the TV productions rather than relegating such activities to a stuntman, he had developed many aches and pains that took its toll on his body. Since I was an orthopedic surgeon, our initial solid conversation was relative to those aches and pains, and I would give him various advice plus medications to meet his needs. This was about the time that the Wrather Corporation in Hollywood (the owners of the *Lassie* television series and other productions) put an injunction on Clayton from wearing the Lone Ranger mask in his shows, as the Wrather Corporation wanted the new and younger Lone Ranger to be the exclusive one. Instead, Clayton wore a wraparound pair of sunglasses, but the effect was not as profound as the mask.

I was Clayton's constant source of encouragement when he was not on the road, and we did become good friends, even to the point that I became his part-time advisor. For example, Clayton did his tours in an underpowered pickup truck with an oversized camper on the back, which hung over the sides of the truck bed like a pendulous belly of a fat man. The additional problem was frequent breakdowns, particularly when driving through the mountains. After I gained his confidence, I explained that he needed an eight-cylinder engine instead of his underpowered six-cylinder to get through the mountains out west. As for his "fat man" living facility in the back of the truck, I pointed out two things that were needed, the first being a double rear axle instead of the anemic job that he did have, plus a truck with a bigger bed to hold the oversized camper.

Well, he listened to me and fulfilled all three of my recommendations. Right about this time he won the countersuit against the Wrather Corporation and could afford the upgrades to his vehicle. He continued his shows until his retirement, moving to Calabasas, California, and I continued to communicate with him for several more years.

I really never knew the fantasy background of the Lone Ranger until I looked it up in the encyclopedia after Clayton's death in 1999. I had not known that he was the alleged sole survivor of a Texas Ranger posse that had been ambushed by outlaws. I knew a fair bit about the Lone Ranger's faithful companion Tonto, played by Jay Silverheels, as Clayton and I had talked about him on several occasions. Clayton had great respect for Jay, and in the films and TV shows Tonto called the Lone Ranger "ke-mo sah-bee," a phrase reportedly derived from a Native American term meaning "trusted friend."

Clayton hit the Hollywood Walk of Fame in 1987, and as of 2006 he was the only person on the Hollywood Walk of Fame to have his character's name along with his real name on the star, which reads, "Clayton Moore – The Lone Ranger." Clayton died in 1999. My oldest son Mark went to the memorial ceremony at the Gene Autry Museum in Los Angeles, and I'm pleased to say that he took my memorabilia to the ceremony as a donation for the museum.

I will say that I've had very few good friends in my lifetime, but I truly place Clayton in that circle. We both taught each other many good points of living and surviving.

Elizabeth Taylor

I was a first-year orthopedic doctor in training at the Harvard/Massachusetts General Hospital in Boston in 1957, and part of my duties was to do the pre-operative physical evaluations on the scheduled surgical patients.

I reported to my duty station on a sunny Tuesday morning and the unit head nurse said to me, "You will like this one." No name was rendered.

So with my neatly pressed white uniform and little black bag, I knocked on the assigned door and a very sweet voice responded, "Come in," and I did.

Well, sitting on the side of the bed was this living doll, and I had never seen such beautiful eyes in all my life, blue/purple with sparkling white speckles. My constitution was simply not geared for this encounter.

We exchanged greetings and, after explaining to Elizabeth Taylor the purpose of my intrusion, I took the toys out of my doctor bag and nervously placed them on the nightstand. She was very kind in her responses. She stayed seated on the side of the bed, perfectly placed for the encounter. After taking a few additional glances at those gorgeous eyes, I placed the ear speculum in her left ear, then withdrew the speculum and smiled, and she smiled in return. I repeated the procedure on the right ear with an equal response. I did not have the nerve to look into her nose, so that was passed up.

The next target was her throat, and that involved protrusion of the tongue, but that was no problem, and subsequently I smiled and she smiled in return. The palpation of her neck was exhilarating, and thankfully no goiter masses were found. I next nervously lowered her gown enough to give audience to the stethoscope, and again I smiled, and again she smiled in return. I nervously picked up the stethoscope and placed it on the left side of her upper chest, listened intently for a few moments then repeated the process three times, as the stethoscope migrated to the right side of her upper chest. With the fourth application, Elizabeth took the earpieces of the stethoscope, which were still around my neck, and appropriately placed them in my ears. She smiled and I blushed. Have you ever felt like a penny waiting for change?

Well, I didn't have enough sense to say nothing about this encounter, as later I told the scenario to the head nurse. Within one hour the story was all over the hospital, and over the next year I received multiple commentaries. At times some employees just looked at me and smiled or laughed, and I knew what they were thinking.

Elvis Presley

I had been the first orthopedic consultant to the St. Croix Falls Wisconsin Hospital and Clinic in about 1965 when I was asked to see a patient at a rehabilitation center on my route to St. Croix Falls from my office in Minneapolis. I was told that it was a celebrity but I was in a hurry at the time and did not pursue the issue. I was also told that the problem was not major or urgent and therefore I did not pursue an immediate resolution.

So four days later I arrived at the Hazelden Rehabilitation Center and had the privilege of meeting Elvis Presley. I say privilege, since I soon appreciated that he was truly a neat guy. Now, his orthopedic problem falls into the Mickey Mouse category and will not be discussed, and also the issue of patient confidentiality presents itself, but on my second visit to the facility he gave me additional information which I had not solicited. He told me that his addiction was Valium and that he had both the physical and mental complications of the same. I actually did not know about the physical problems associated with Valium, but soon learned that chronic and significant Valium use creates non-skeletal muscle degeneration. I had also long forgotten that the heart consists of non-skeletal muscle, and therefore degeneration could produce congestive cardiac failure. I personally felt related to the issue, since I had survived severe cardiac failure at age nine secondary to rheumatic heart disease. Instead of dying at the hospital to which I was sent, I walked out of the facility fourteen months later, the entire scenario having been classified a miracle.

Elvis told me that he was not so lucky and asked me to get the word out that Valium can kill. So why did it take me so long? It is very simple, I really had no reasonable or acceptable mechanism to do so, and I was extremely busy at the time and did not spend the effort necessary to develop the scenario which he recommended.

We became acquainted enough such that he invited me to Sound 80 Studios in Minneapolis, where he made two recordings. At the time I was making fire and police training films in Minneapolis, and instead of being in the room where he recorded, I was learning to use the Grass Valley Switchboard, doing the technical adjustments at the time he was recording.

I really felt bad when he died at age forty-two, shortly after I had attended one of his performances in Las Vegas. He had truly one of the greatest male voices I had ever heard. I particularly enjoyed his religious music, and to this day I know of no other male singer who attains that level of perfection in performance. I regret not having cultured the acquaintance.

Arthur Godfrey

It was 1957 and I was a Harvard orthopedic resident physician (in training) at Massachusetts General Hospital in Boston when I was told to do a preoperative physical on a "guy" in the Phillips house (which we reverently called the "P" house). I showed up in my white uniform and with my little black bag and asked the name and room number of the victim. I was told that it was radio and television entertainer Arthur Godfrey and that "no one can please him." Well, I felt I would go for broke.

I pounded on the door and received the warm welcome of, "Who the hell is it?"

I opened the door, put my black bag on the foot of the bed and said, "I want to buy one of your damn airplanes."

He said, "What the hell do you know about my airplanes?"

I replied, "You have three Ford tri-motor planes and I can run faster on the ground than they can fly in the air."

He responded with, "Sit down, kid, and let's talk."

Well, the talking lasted one and a half hours and a crowd had gathered outside the door, fearing I had been murdered. While I gave Mr. Godfrey the specifications of the engines of his planes plus other statistics, he asked how I ever got such knowledge. I told him that before the Air Force was formed I wanted to go to West Point and be a fighter pilot in the army. However, I wore glasses and was not accepted. I furthermore told him that I had boarded a bus, went up to the Coast Guard Academy in New London, Connecticut and was accepted to the academy. However, the war ended shortly thereafter, so I decided to play doctor the rest of my life.

In our discussions Arthur mentioned his desire to fly a P-51 fighter plane, so I gave him the history of the twelve-cylinder P-51 and told him that when the Rolls Royce Company couldn't meet our demand, we moved on to Pratt Whitney engines. I also explained that the original cockpits had visual impairment and so we went to the bubble. Since he had not flown a P-51 yet, I cautioned him not to touch the throttle while the plane was on the runway and until the plane was in the air, so as not to spin the fuselage. His response was, "I can't believe this kid."

Arthur invited me to his ranch after he would recover from having cup arthroplasties to both hips, the predecessor to the total hip replacement. I would have loved to accept the invitation, but I continued my one hundred miles-per-hour-life without limitation or abatement.

Wilt the Stilt

It was 1957 and my first year at the Harvard/MGH orthopedic resident training program. First-year residents were called the "Pups," which meant they got not only the menial chores, but also the more senior residents enjoyed pulling tricks on the newer guys.

I had on my little white suit, carrying my little black bag and walking to the clinic to start the day's chores when I was told there was a basketball player to be seen who had gotten into a fight the night before in the Boston Gardens with Bob Cousy. I was to examine and treat the basketball player.

I watched this guy come into the clinic. He was so tall that he had to duck his head under the exposed overhead pipes, and he was placed in a cubicle to which I was directed. It didn't take long for me to recognize Wilt "The Stilt" Chamberlain of the Harlem Globetrotters, and it was my job to evaluate the swelling of his right hand at the base of the knuckle.

This very tall individual took one look at me and said, "Is you a real docta?" Even though I was twenty-seven years old, I knew that I looked like I was about sixteen.

My response to Wilt was, "No, I work at a meat market down the road but they let me come in here on Tuesday mornings to play doctor in the clinic."

Wilt laughed but responded by asking me, "Does you have any kids?" When I responded in the affirmative, he asked me whether my kids looked older than I did.

We did get down to business and he was very cooperative with both the exam and the x-rays. By this time a crowd had gathered to view the events and eventual x-rays. Wilt was very pleased to see and hear that he did not have a fracture or any major injury to the hand. We actually got along quite well, passing back and forth a few other points of humor, Wilt playing right along with the whole game.

I had fun with the x-rays at the very serious conservative orthopedic weekly grand rounds at Massachusetts General Hospital. Initially the viewers were of the impression that I had taken a magnification x-ray by holding the hand about two inches away from the x-ray plate, until they realized that this huge hand was that of Wilt the Stilt.

Although I did not follow Wilt's remaining career because of my busy schedule, I remained interested in basketball and did take note that he went from the Harlem Globetrotters to the Philadelphia 76ers. He also had created quite a sensation in the Soviet Union when, actually as a Globetrotter, the Russians simply could not figure out what these guys were doing. The benefit was they took along their own competition, because the Soviet players never could have dealt with such circus type of gymnastics. It is certainly a thrill to know that guys like Wilt went on to inspire many young kids who otherwise would not have had that ray of hope or light in their lives, and for such we are forever thankful and grateful to everything that Wilt had done to entertain us. Also, he is the only NBA player to achieve one hundred points in a single game, a great goal for the kids playing basketball to attempt to achieve or duplicate.

Don Shula
It was 1950 in Cleveland, Ohio at John Carroll University when I was privileged to live in the Jesuit resident building, Rodman Hall, because of my grades and behavior (another miracle). It just so happened that two rooms down on the same floor were the two stars of our football team; Don Shula and Carl Taseff. Believe it or not, Don served early morning mass for the Jesuit priests in Rodman Hall. He allegedly had that angelic aura, but let me tell you the other side of the story.

In the room next to mine was Father Horvath, a Jesuit priest who had recently been let out of a communist prison in Hungary. He was a nervous wreck and so my roommate and I never played the radio loud. Well, Shula and Taseff, party boys, "borrowed" a mannequin from the May Company Department Store in downtown Cleveland. They propped the mannequin up on the toilet in one of the bathroom stalls across the hall from Father Horvath's room, and then pounded on the metal walls of the stall, yelling some type of gibberish. Poor Father Horvath came stumbling from his room and into the bathroom, half dressed, shaking and screaming, particularly when he saw what was propped up on the toilet.

I heard the commotion and ran into the bathroom, then carefully escorted Father Horvath, still shaking, back to his room. Now guess who was down the hall laughing hysterically? Yes, the two angels of ill repute.

Now, Don Shula may be the winningest and greatest professional coach of all time, but everyone has some skeletons in their closets—or in this case, mannequins in their toilet stalls.

Emile Grubbe

It was in 1957 when I was a general surgery resident training physician at St. Francis Hospital in Evanston, Illinois. I would proceed to and from my apartment to the hospital in my little white suit, so obviously my destination was apparent. I was recently married and lived in an eight-plex on the third floor, going up and down daily on the elevator. On several occasions I encountered a man wearing many bandages on his face and hands. I had also seen this man at the clinic in the hospital, and therefore a verbal encounter was easy. After about the third brief greeting, the gentleman invited me to come to his apartment for a visit. I did arrange for such an encounter. He lived alone and I soon found out that he was Dr. Emile Grubbe, the first physician to use x-ray in the treatment of cancer, and without any protection for either the provider or patients.

Dr. Grubbe informed me that he was both a chemist and a homeopathic physician, and that he had been the first American to use radiation in the treatment of cancer patients. Needless to say, the absence of protective devices produced profound complications for both the physician providing the treatment as well as the recipient patients.

Emile admitted that he just needed somebody to talk to, so he gave me the history of the first x-ray machine—that being produced in 1896 at Hahnemann Medical College of Philadelphia–and said that during his own career he had assembled his x-ray machine only one year after Wilhelm Roentgen discovered the x-ray itself. Emile had ultimately treated over ninety patients for cancer with his radiation apparatus, and some of those patients also had been seen at St. Francis Hospital, as a very prominent plastic surgeon practiced at that facility and even had the contract from the State of Illinois to treat severely burned children.

We had several visits before I went on to my orthopedic residency training program at Harvard/Massachusetts General Hospital in Boston, and I still remember the endless hours of taking care of burn patients at St. Francis using ether and debriding the wounds. These were the days before the magic ointment Silvadene had been developed, and therefore we had no shortcuts to the prolonged process of treating these patients.

In preparing this segment, I looked up Emile Grubbe on Wikipedia and found the scenario to be absolutely fascinating. On reflection, I must admit that Emile Grubbe made me both think and weep.

Les Paul and Mary Ford

I was fifteen years old and returning to my second year of reform school in Wisconsin when a friend from the first year invited me to come a couple days earlier to Chicago and see the town. Well, I accepted the invitation only to find that my friend's father owned the Blue Note Café on Michigan Avenue in Chicago, starring the husband and wife musical team of Les Paul and Mary Ford.

While I was too young to drink alcohol, I was fascinated by this duo who made vibratory music come out of their guitars that literally rocked the woodwork. First of all, Mary Ford was a doll. That was an attraction in itself, plus she had a neat, smooth and seductive voice.

On the second night of attending the club, I asked the couple how they initially got the idea of the reverberation sound from the guitars. They told me of the earlier days when they did their recordings in a shower room after getting the moisture up to a maximum level. I thought that was quite ingenious, as I had finally found someone more diabolical than myself.

Mary Ford died at age fifty-three, a true loss to the musical world. I am not a music nut, but this lady captivated me (admittedly I am weak). I remember her radio broadcast on Friday nights, especially when I was a ranger, and either Mary Ford or the "Lonesome Gal" (Jean King) were our choice. I must admit that "How High the Moon" and the "Tennessee Waltz" won out. I later learned that the multi-tracking sound actually came from recording in a mountain cave. How is that for ingenuity?

Les Paul was a marvel and a legend. In 1951 he and Mary sold more recordings than Bing Crosby, Frank Sinatra, and the Andrew Sisters combined. I lost track of Les until October of 2009 when I asked a music professor from the music school next to my office what had happened to Les. He told me that Les had died only a few months prior to that time at the age of ninety-four, and that he had played at the Nirvana Nightclub in New York on Monday evenings until age ninety-two. I later learned that it was the Iridium Jazz Club. (And people think that I'm a relic for still working at age eighty-seven.)

Carol Channing

It was in the mid-1960s when I attended a party at the home of my next-door neighbor Sandy Fawcett, who was a leading figure in the Boys and Girls Club of Minneapolis. The honored guest was Carol Channing, whom I had seen in *Hello Dolly* just two nights before at the Orpheum Theater in Minneapolis. Carol was apparently very involved in the Boys and Girls Club in America, and the party was a tribute to her contribution.

Well, I assumed a very passive role (hard to believe) and just watched the performance, and it was quite a show. Carol was at the piano most of the time just playing and singing. To my surprise, she sounded just like she did on the stage; the piercing, beautiful tones were her natural voice. I admit I was thoroughly entertained. I'm equally thrilled to know that she is still alive and active at the age of ninety-six at the time of this writing. I must say that that evening was just one of those choice, memorable moments that one enjoys recalling.

However, in writing this segment I decided to explore Carol's journey since the time of my personal interface at the party. I had seen her in *Hello Dolly* but had forgotten about *Gentlemen Prefer Blondes* and *Thoroughly Modern Millie*. Wikipedia let me know that she had achieved the American Theater Hall of Fame in 1981 (truly deserved). I also learned that *Hello Dolly* was for a time the longest running musical in Broadway history (no big surprise).

Other items of interest: She was married four times (beat me by one); she was the first celebrity to perform at a Super Bowl halftime in 1970; and she was on President Nixon's "enemy list." The item that really lit my fire was the report that she brought her own food into restaurants, refusing to eat menu items. (Now I can see a personality trait I can relate to. See, I'm not the only unique creature.)

Pete Fountain

When I was in my twenties I had very little time for entertainment, but I did enjoy some music. One of my favorite musicians was Pete Fountain, as I had never heard anyone produce such beautiful sounds out of a clarinet previously. Periodically I would buy his records or CDs, depending on the era.

Sometime in my mid-forties I was in New Orleans and dining with an individual who was attempting to convince me to relocate to Atlanta, so we were in deep discussions. The restaurant was on Bourbon Street, and being a weeknight, not unusually crowded.

I did notice a man sitting alone at a table across the room. After finishing his glass of wine, he threw the empty glass around the corner, shattering the glass against the wall. Needless to say, a crash resulted, and I was shocked.

My dinner companion and I returned to our discussion, and about twenty minutes later the same scenario recurred. This time I asked the waiter what was going on, since the other customers (obviously regulars) did not seem perturbed. The waiter informed me that the gentleman was Pete Fountain, a popular jazz clarinetist, and that the scenario was not that uncommon. Since I knew Mr. Fountain owned his own restaurant down the street, I asked the waiter why Mr. Fountain did not patronize his own facility and behave in a similar fashion. I was informed that, "No, he likes it here." So I went back to my discussions.

After Pete died in 2016, I looked up his history on the internet and was surprised to learn that he started playing the clarinet as a teenager at the recommendation of his physician as a therapeutic measure in dealing with a chronic lung problem. The suggestion sure paid off, as Pete had listened to recordings of Benny Goodman to perfect his style and ultimately ended up playing with famous trumpeter Al Hirt at Dan Levy's Pier 600. Not a bad career for a kid with a chronic lung problem.

Rex Humbard

I was a teenager and living in a two-story house at 1716 - 14th Street in Cuyahoga Falls, Ohio when, as the house was for sale, a red convertible containing television evangelist Rex Humbard and a real estate agent pulled up in front.

Now, we had two movie theaters in Cuyahoga Falls, the Falls Theatre on Front Street and the Ohio Theatre on State Road. The latter was purchased by Rev. Rex Humbard and converted into a Pentecostal musical church, which included Rex being the wizard on the guitar, a red-hot support team, and a woman who had a very angelic and direct voice.

Within weeks of the church's opening, lines were out to the street, and multiple interim service facilities were developed for the expanding demand, ultimately manifesting its explosive growth in the fifty-four hundred-seat facility called the Cathedral of Tomorrow in Cuyahoga Falls, Ohio. This was the site of the dynamic music related religious services which were soon to spread all over the world.

So where did Rex come from? The short answer is Little Rock, Arkansas. However, he attended church revivals all over the nation, taking the meat and potatoes from each to give him the ultimate concept and manifestations of the Cathedral of Tomorrow. Although I did not attend the church services, I did enjoy the cafeteria.

I also enjoyed watching the construction of his hoped-for worldwide cement tower, intended for international transmission with a restaurant on top. The structure went belly-up when the ministry got into financial difficulties with securities and private ventures. The kids of Cuyahoga Falls nicknamed the structure "The Tower of Babble," not to be confused with the "Tower of Babel," which allegedly had been built in ancient Middle East.

When I had seen Elvis Presley at Hazelden, a drug and alcohol treatment facility, he asked me if I knew Rex, and I responded in the negative. Elvis relayed to me that it was Rex who inspired him to delve into religious music, and I must admit it was Elvis's religious music that I enjoyed the most. As things developed, Rex presided over the service at Elvis's funeral, another event that I missed.

It is reported that Rex's worldwide ministry touched over eight million humans per weekend, so he was the top of the deck. His business developments ranged from the sublime to the ridiculous, which probably meets the format of most of our lives.

Humbard was inducted into the Broadcasting Hall of Fame in 1983, being classified by the *U.S. News & World Report* as one of the "Top 25 principal architects of the American Century." Since my father was a true architect by trade, I did not see the connection.

There were spinoffs of the cathedral in both Cuyahoga Falls and Canton, Ohio, but many of the financial problems were never fully resolved, resulting in the collapse of several aspects of both the direct and indirect ventures of the church. However, many of his followers raised $12-million to soften the blow of the reduction.

Rex Humbard died in 2007 at the age of eighty-eight in Atlantis, Florida with several family members continuing to carry the torch; however, there was no doubt that Rex Humbard was a pioneer in radio and TV musical ministry.

Kate Smith and Ted Collins

It was just after World War II, which meant I didn't have to work all summer, and a high school classmate named Jim Krill had a new convertible. So we decided to take a mini vacation to upper New York and ended up in the Adirondack Mountains at a town called Saranac.

We were sitting in the theater watching a very exciting movie, which I thought was *Crossfire* but have been told since that the timeframe does not fit. In any case, there was a sizable lady sitting in front of me with a large hat, and I was dodging from side to side trying to avoid the hat and see the movie.

Ultimately I asked the lady if she would please remove her hat. A very familiar voice said, "Oh, I am very sorry," and the movie immediately became more visible for me. After the production was completed, the lady stood up, turned around and it was obviously Kate Smith, known as the First Lady of Radio in the United States during the Second World War. With her was Ted Collins, her business manager for thirty years, and she smiled at me and apologized before proceeding to exit the theater.

Kate walked to her multi-tan Oldsmobile station wagon wearing a knee-level skirt (I had always seen her on the TV in a long skirt), and I do remember her very muscular calves in the shorter garment. I blurted out, "America loves you," and she readily responded, "Thank you very much," and proceeded to enter her vehicle. I was told that Kate and Ted lived on an island in the middle of Saranac Lake, and that was obviously their destination at this late hour in the evening. I truly have fond memories of that very brief encounter, as World War II did have a significant psychological effect upon myself as a teenager.

Xavier Cugat and Abbe Lane

I was in third year medical school in Chicago, and always willing to pick up some spending money, when my classmate Wally asked me to be the gofer at a party for famous bandleader Xavier Cugat in his apartment at the Edgewater Beach Hotel on the North Shore of Chicago. Cugat's Saturday night radio shows from the hotel were a classic in America, especially since Abbe Lane was his "bird" (another description for a singer). Being from Spain, Cugat popularized Spanish music around America just as Frankie Yankovic did for the polka out of Cleveland. However, Cugat's bird, his fourth wife, was a real ticket as she could both tweet and wiggle. Their apartment was in the building next to the hotel, and I soon learned how to carry the juices and food up the four floors in the back of the building. It was hard work, but it was worth it. As the party progressed, she pealed down like an onion, even bringing tears to my eyes. Throughout the entire procedure she always held her little Chihuahua, which surprisingly wasn't offended by all the attention. As the onion got thinner, the attendees cheered louder. It was a memorable treat.

Cugat was actually born in Spain and was named after St. Francis of Assisi, but I think he left his sainthood behind. However, he truly introduced the nation to Spanish music. It caught on and fitted well, particularly with the influx of the people from Mexico, truly a delightful culture.

Shari Lewis

Seeing puppets on TV today is routine, not only in children's programs but extensively in commercials, and now even dovetailed in regular scripting. Yet, it wasn't always that way. Early puppets were just that, namely someone's hand shoved inside the visible puppet while the activation was hidden, usually below the sightline, and the voice was that of the puppeteer.

In the middle 1960s I was making medical training films for firemen and policemen with a film producer in the Twin Cities, and an associate of that producer invited me to view a proposed production with Shari Lewis, the famed puppeteer, along with her buddy, Lamb Chop the puppet. The film was to be titled, *Hush Puppy's Bright Idea*. I don't remember much about the content, but the film was primarily for education for children's safety. We did have a lot of fun making the show. Shari had truly a magnetic and charming personality. I was left with some very fond memories, and it was truly enjoyable to be a part of the birth of an industry.

Mother Teresa

It was in the early 1970s that I was asked to be the bodyguard of Mother Teresa for the three-day seminar that she was to give to her coworkers from all over the nation. It was to occur in Bloomington, Minnesota, a suburb of Minneapolis.

Why me? Well, my wife at the time was the number two coworker in the Mother Teresa Organization, and the number one coworker in the United States was the wife of one of my associates in medical practice. Both he and I were to assume the duties of "bodyguard" for Mother Teresa, but in reality it merely meant crowd control. However, since at the time I was also associated with the Minnesota Highway Patrol, I knew that religious fanatics did exist.

Warren and I were very careful of who came in and out of the area surrounding Mother Teresa. Interestingly enough, when her plane landed at a private terminal of the Minneapolis airport, several young people spotted her and came out to greet and touch her. We were of a heightened alert status, but no problems arose.

The two-and-a-half-day seminar was a basic learning experience, and it was obvious that this lady was of a very highly spiritual level, clearly being a recipient of God's abundant graces and powers. I learned much in those two and a half days about the proper perspectives of life and death.

I had only one brief opportunity to talk to Mother Teresa in the group setting, so at the airport when she was waiting for the final servicing of the private plane that was to take her to her next destination, I turned to her and, not knowing what to say, blurted out, "What does God want me to do?"

Her rapid response was, "pray constantly."

I responded by saying, "But I'm not in a convent or monastery," and she snapped back with, "Make it a habit and say these three little words." With that she turned and walked toward the twin-engine Beechcraft aircraft, now ready for takeoff.

I stood there thinking. Since part of my practice at that time was to teach pain patients not to do certain activities or addictive behaviors, I wondered if it was possible to teach myself to do a repetitive thing that could be addicting. I remembered my medical work in Afghanistan and the two incidents that somewhat puzzled me at the time. The first was a man whose prayer beads fell into a sizable crack in the floor of our dilapidated clinic. He actually went through an anxiety attack until we got a pair of surgical forceps and retrieved the entrapped beads. His anxiety immediately disappeared.

The second incident was another patient in the clinic who had also misplaced his prayer beads and was screaming frantically. We all stopped working and turned the clinic upside down until we found the beads, and immediately his screaming and weeping stopped. They were both obviously addicted to the prayer beads and the prayers.

I never forgot those two incidents, which I classified as addiction to prayer while requiring the prayer beads. So I decided to try the experiment of becoming addicted to the three words given to me by Mother Teresa. On the first day I said the three little words on the hour for about thirty seconds. The next day I expanded the exercise to say the three words for about one minute on the hour, but because of my schedule considerable variation occurred.

I began reciting the three little words whenever my brain and mind was not occupied, and on some days that was very difficult. As time progressed and with persistence in implementing the experiment, it actually happened that I not only became addicted to the three words, but I developed anxiety if my mind was not working or thinking and if I was not saying the three little words.

There was a period of significant absence of the format, but in 2015 I resumed the effort and now have the full addiction accompanied by anxiety in its absence. I must admit that there is a calming element to this addiction and, being of advanced age, I contemplate that if I can't get into the front or back door of heaven, I'm hoping Mother Teresa will let me in the basement window, reciting those three little words.

Several years ago Mother Teresa mailed to me, in response to a donation for her work a handwritten note with the following: "A physician must give of himself until he dies, and when he ceases to give, he is dead."

So if I get to heaven before you do, I will hold the door open for your entrance.

If you say those three little words.

THE END